Managing the Risk of Workplace Stress

Working in a stressful environment not only increases the risk of physical illness or distress, but also increases the likelihood of workplace accidents. While legislation provides some guidelines for risk assessment of physical hazards, there remains limited guidance on the risks of psychosocial hazards, such as occupational stress.

Managing the Risk of Workplace Stress takes a risk management approach to stress evaluation in the workplace, offering practical guidelines for the audit, assessment and mitigation of workplace stressors. Based on original research findings, it provides a comprehensive source of theoretical and practical information for students and practitioners alike.

The book includes chapters on:

- Environmental safety factors
- Psychological safety factors
- Job stress and work-related accidents
- Risk assessment methods
- Risk evaluation.

With its up-to-date approach to a fascinating area of study, *Managing the Risk of Workplace Stress* is key reading for all students of organizational psychology and those responsible for workplace safety.

Sharon Clarke is Lecturer in Organizational Psychology at UMIST.

Cary L. Cooper CBE is Professor of Organizational Psychology and Health at the Lancaster University Management School, Lancaster University.

Managing the Risk of Workplace Stress

Health and safety hazards

Sharon Clarke and
Cary L. Cooper

Taylor & Francis Group

LONDON AND NEW YORK

First published 2004
by Routledge
11 New Fetter Lane, London EC4P 4EE

Simultaneously published in the USA and Canada
by Routledge
29 West 35th Street, New York, NY 10001

Routledge is an imprint of the Taylor & Francis Group

© 2004 Sharon Clarke and Cary L. Cooper

Typeset in Sabon by
BOOK NOW Ltd
Printed and bound in Great Britain by
TJ International Ltd, Padstow, Cornwall

British Library Cataloguing in Publication Data
A catalogue record for this book is available
from the British Library

Library of Congress Cataloging in Publication Data
Cooper, Cary L.
    Managing the risk of workplace stress / Cary L. Cooper and Sharon Clarke.
        p. cm.
Includes bibliographical references and index.
    1. Job stress. 2. Stress management. 3. Industrial accidents.
4. Work environment–Psychological aspects. I. Clarke, Sharon, 1968–
II. Title.
    HF5548.85.C6556 2004
    658.4'095–dc21   2003014619

ISBN 0–415–29710–9 (hbk)
ISBN 0–415–29709–5 (pbk)

Contents

Illustrations

Acknowledgements

The authors wish to acknowledge all their academic colleagues and students at UMIST who have stimulated thoughts for this book.

For the intellectual leadership and personal support that have contributed greatly to his work throughout his career, Professor Cooper would like to express his special thanks to Professor Lennart Levi of the Karolinska Institute, Sweden.

As always the support of our families is gratefully acknowledged. Dr Clarke would particularly like to thank her husband, Peter Axworthy, and children, Emily Rose and Sam, for their forbearance during the writing of this book.

Chapter 1

Introduction

Working in a stressful environment increases the risk both of suffering physical illness or symptoms of psychological distress (Cooper and Cartwright 1994; Cooper and Payne 1988), and also work-related accidents and injuries (Sutherland and Cooper 1991). The substantive body of well-documented research evidence supporting a causal relationship between working conditions, both physical and psychosocial, and individual health and well-being, has legitimised the concept of stress-induced illness and disease. Although it has received less academic interest, there is also research evidence supporting causal links between stressful working conditions and greater accident involvement in various contexts, including company car drivers (Cartwright *et al.* 1996), transit operators (Greiner *et al.* 1998), medical practitioners (Kirkcaldy *et al.* 1997) and veterinary surgeons (Trimpop *et al.* 2000).

In an increasingly litigious society, recent years have seen a growing number of 'cumulative trauma' compensation claims against US employers (National Institute of Occupational Safety and Health (NIOSH) 1986); Karasek and Theorell 1990), and later, a number of successful personal injury claims in the United Kingdom (Earnshaw and Cooper 2001). The concept of 'cumulative trauma' relates to the development of mental illness as a result of continual exposure to occupational stress; the California Labor Code states that workers are entitled to compensation for disability or illness caused by 'repetitive mentally or physically traumatic activities extending over a period of time, the combined effect of which causes any disability or need for medical treatment'. In the United Kingdom, the legal implications of stress-induced personal injury were highlighted by the landmark case of *Walker* v *Northumberland County Council* (see Box 1.1).

Box 1.1 The John Walker case

John Walker worked for Northumberland County Council from 1970 until December 1987 as an area social services officer. He held a middle-management position and was responsible for four teams of social services fieldworkers in the Blyth Valley area. Mr Walker was responsible for allocating cases to teams of field social workers and for holding case conferences in respect of children referred to his area of the Social Services Department. During the 1980s the population of Blyth Valley rose, leading to an increase in the volume of work to be undertaken by Mr Walker and his teams, but there was no corresponding rise in the number of fieldworkers. Mr Walker and his teams were increasingly under pressure, and this, of itself and apart from the stressful nature of the work, created stress and anxiety.

Between 1985 and 1987, Mr Walker repeatedly complained (in writing) to his superiors, expressing the need to alleviate the work pressure to which he and his social workers were subject. Mr Walker requested a redistribution of resources from rural areas to urban areas, such as his own. In November 1985, Mr Walker told his superior, Mr Davidson, that the Blyth Valley area should be split in two, and that he did not think he could go on shouldering his then volume of work. Mr Davidson told Mr Walker he was unwilling to make changes at that point, because within two years there was to be a restructuring of social services in the county. Mr Walker indicated that in that case he could go on, but he could not go on beyond two years. During 1986 the workload continued to increase and in November 1986 Mr Walker suffered a nervous breakdown.

In March 1987, Mr Walker returned to work, having negotiated for assistance to be provided for him on his return. However, support was provided only on an intermittent basis and was withdrawn by early April. During his absence a substantial backlog of paperwork had built up, which took Mr Walker until May to clear. In the meantime the number of pending cases continued to increase and Mr Walker began to experience stress symptoms again. By September 1987 he was advised to go on sick leave and was diagnosed as affected by a state of stress-related anxiety. He suffered a second mental breakdown and was obliged to retire from his post for reasons of ill-health.

Source: adapted from Earnshaw and Cooper (2001).

The judge held that the council was liable for Mr Walker's second nervous breakdown, but not for his first. In this case, the judge expressed the view that the employer's duty of care extended beyond physical injury to 'psychiatric damage' and that the employer 'has a duty to provide his employee with a reasonably safe system of work and to take reasonable steps to protect him from risks which are reasonably foreseeable'. Earnshaw and Cooper (2001) note that, under English law, employers cannot avoid liability due to the particular susceptibility of individuals, once they are aware of such susceptibility: 'once employers are put on notice that a given individual is susceptible to psychiatric harm, they will be liable if it is foreseeable in the circumstances that that individual will suffer such harm' (Earnshaw and Cooper 2001: 47). A number of international bodies have recognised the potential harmful effects of stressful working environments, including the World Health Organisation (WHO) and the International Labour Organisation (ILO).

Cox and Griffiths (1996) argue that organisations need to assess the risk posed by 'psychosocial hazards' as well as physical hazards. Psychosocial hazards are 'those aspects of work design, and the organisation and management of work, and their social and organisational contexts, which have the potential for causing psychological or physical harm' (Cox et al. 1993, 1995). Although much legislation governing health and safety requires risk assessment of the effects of physical hazards on health and safety outcomes, more recently attention has been focused on assessing the risk of psychosocial hazards on health outcomes (Cox et al. 1995; Cox and Griffiths 1996). In 1993 the European Framework Directive on Health and Safety at Work stated that the employer has 'a duty to ensure the safety and health of workers in every aspect related to the work', although a minority of European countries have special legislation relating to psychosocial hazards.

Despite the increased awareness of the potentially harmful effects of occupational stress and psychosocial hazards, the focus has been largely directed at physical and psychological health and well-being. There has been little emphasis on the physical effects of psychosocial hazards, in terms of work-related accidents and occupational injuries. Although there is an assumption within many models of stress that frequent and/or severe accidents are a behavioural outcome of stressful working conditions, there is little explicit discussion of the relationship between occupational stress and work-related accidents. When the full range of negative implications are considered both in terms of ill-health and occupational injuries, the business costs associated with occupational stress are extremely high.

Costs associated with occupational stress

Employees are increasing aware of the impact that occupational stress is having on their work, health and well-being. The International Social Survey Program, conducted in fifteen OECD countries, found that 80 per cent of employees report being stressed at work (OECD 1999). The UK Health and Safety Executive (HSE) estimates that 20 per cent of employees admit to taking time off work because of work-related stress and 8 per cent consult their general practitioner on stress-related problems (Earnshaw and Cooper 2001). A survey on working conditions by the European Foundation for the Improvement of Living and Working Conditions showed that 57 per cent of European workers consider their health is negatively affected by work and 28 per cent felt that their health and safety was at risk (Paoli 1997). Occupational or workplace stress accounts for a high proportion of sickness absence. The HSE estimates that 60 per cent of all work absences are caused by stress-related illnesses, totalling 40 million working days per year (Earnshaw and Cooper 2001). Schabracq *et al.* (1996) estimate that about half of all work absences are stress-related. The costs associated with sickness absence are high, for example, the Confederation of British Industry (CBI) estimates that in financial terms, sickness absence costs some £11 billion per year in the United Kingdom, of which it has been estimated that about 40 per cent is due to workplace stress. This amounts to approximately 2–3 per cent of gross national product (GNP), or £438 per employee per year (CBI 2000).

It is estimated that occupational stress is involved in 60–80 per cent of accidents at work (Sutherland and Cooper 1991). When work accidents and injuries are included, the costs associated with occupational stress escalate further. Although in the United States alone, 65,000 people die each year from work-related injuries and illnesses (Herbert and Landrigan 2000), work-related fatalities are relatively rare, compared to the numbers of employees injured at work, who subsequently take sickness absence. Dupre (2000) estimated that in approximately 50 per cent of work accidents that occurred in Europe (in 1996) absence from work ranged between two weeks and three months. In Australia the average absence for compensated injuries was two months in the period 1998–9 (National Occupational Health and Safety Commission 2000). It is estimated that 80 million working days were lost in the United States due to workplace accidents in 1998 (US Bureau of the Census 2000). Work accidents are damaging not only for those involved, but also for their employers. Work injuries cost Americans $131.2 billion in 2000, a figure that exceeds the combined profits of the top 13 Fortune 500 companies (National Safety Council 2001). In the United Kingdom, it has been estimated that work accidents cost employers £3–7 billion per year, equivalent to approximately 4–8 per cent of all UK industrial and commercial companies' gross trading profits (Health and Safety Executive 1999).

This brief overview indicates the enormity of the costs associated with stress-related illness and accidents, and highlights the potential benefits of successfully managing the risks of occupational stress. There are often hidden business costs that are incurred as a result of work-related illness and injuries, including the costs of training and recruitment of temporary cover for absent employees.

The nature of occupational stress

Contemporary definitions of stress tend to favour a transactional perspective; this emphasises that stress is located neither in the person nor in the environment, but in the relationship between the two (Cooper *et al.* 2001). Within this perspective the term 'stress' refers to the overall transactional process, not to specific elements, such as the individual or the environment. Stress arises when the demands of a particular encounter are appraised by the individual as about to exceed the available resources and, therefore, threaten well-being, and necessitate a change in individual functioning to restore the imbalance (Lazarus 1991). *Stressors* refer to the events that are encountered by individuals, while *strain* refers to the individual's psychological, physical and behavioural responses to stressors (Beehr 1998).

Stressors

Sources of occupational stress were categorised by Cooper and Marshall (1976) as intrinsic to the job; role in the organisation; relationships at work; career development; organisational structure and climate; home–work interface (see Figure 1.1). These broad categories have been supported by later research, including Cox (1993) and Cartwright and Cooper (1997). Those that are 'intrinsic to the job' will include physical aspects of the working environment, such as noise and lighting, and psychosocial aspects, such as workload, and will vary in importance depending on the job, e.g. health care professionals experience high workload, the need to work long hours, time pressures and inadequate free time (e.g. Wolfgang 1988; Sutherland and Cooper 1990); while money-handling and the threat of violence at work are stressors for bus drivers (Duffy and McGoldrick 1990). Sources of pressure are derived not only from factors inherent in the job itself, but also from the organisational context, such as the structure and climate of the organisation (e.g. management style, level of consultation, communication and politics). Research shows that organisational stressors can have more impact, even in seemingly 'stressful' jobs, than factors intrinsic to the job, e.g. the police (Hart *et al.* 1995) and teaching occupations (Hart 1994). Hart *et al.* (1995) found that hassles associated with police organisations (e.g. communication,

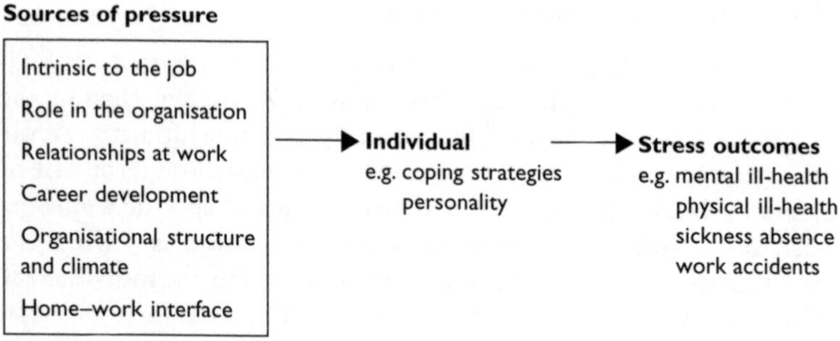

Sources of pressure

| Intrinsic to the job |
| Role in the organisation |
| Relationships at work |
| Career development |
| Organisational structure and climate |
| Home–work interface |

⟶ **Individual**
e.g. coping strategies
personality

⟶ **Stress outcomes**
e.g. mental ill-health
physical ill-health
sickness absence
work accidents

Figure 1.1 The occupational stress model.
Source: adapted from Cooper and Marshall (1976).

administration) were the main predictor of psychological distress among police officers.

Sparks and Cooper (1999) emphasise the need to measure a broad range of stressors, in order to reflect specific situations. A number of empirical studies have found that job-specific stressors are important in predicting outcomes for particular occupations (e.g. anaesthetists; Cooper *et al.* 1999), and that generic stressors vary between occupational groups (Sparks and Cooper 1999). Furthermore, significant differences have been found between work groups and departments within organisations, reflecting perceptions of different subcultures (Cooper and Bramwell 1992).

Sparks *et al.* (2001) identify four sources of stress of particular importance, due to the changing nature of the modern business world: job insecurity, work hours, control at work and managerial style. Recent trends in working practices across Europe have witnessed an increase in work pace (Paoli 1997) and the emergence of alternative work schedules, with some workers completing work shifts in excess of eight hours (Rosa 1995), while others work compressed schedules so that a working week of 36–48 hours is completed in three or four days (Sparks *et al.* 2001). In Europe, it is an increasingly common practice to base work schedules on weekly, monthly or yearly work hours (Brewster *et al.* 1996). Although EU legislation on working hours (European Commission Working Time Directive 1990) has resulted in a slight decline in annual work hours, in other countries, particularly where labour markets have been deregulated (e.g. United Kingdom, United States, New Zealand) work hours have increased (Bosch 1999). The OECD (1999) survey found that 35 per cent of UK employees work more than 40 hours per week. A meta-analytic review of the literature found significant relationships between long work hours and employees' mental and physical ill-health (Sparks *et al.* 1997).

Cooper (1999) notes that the psychological contract between employer and employee is being undermined to the extent that employees increasingly no longer regard their work as secure. A European survey (International Survey Research (ISR) 1995) conducted across 400 companies, located in seventeen different countries, revealed that employment security declined significantly between 1985 and 1995. This trend is reflected in employee perceptions of job insecurity, which are having serious effects on health and well-being in European workers (Borg *et al.* 2000; Domenighetti *et al.* 2000). North American employees are experiencing similar effects, for example, McDonough (2000) found that, for Canadian workers, perceived job insecurity was significantly associated with reduced general health and increased psychological distress.

Role of individual factors

Occupational stress has been defined by many researchers (e.g. Cox 1978; Cummings and Cooper 1979; Quick and Quick 1984) as 'a negatively perceived quality which as a result of inadequate coping with sources of stress, has negative mental and physical health consequences'. There are two key dimensions of this definition: in order for an individual to experience stress symptoms, first, the source of stress must be 'negatively perceived', and second, the individual must display 'inadequate coping' (see Figure 1.2).

The experience of stress symptoms is therefore both subjective and dependent on individual differences. If a source of stress is positively perceived, e.g. as a challenge to be overcome, then the individual will not experience negative outcomes. However, some individuals are predisposed to perceive themselves in a negative light, that is, they are high in 'negative affectivity' (Watson and Clark 1984), and are, therefore, more likely to perceive job situations as stressful. Research studies have found that individuals high in negative affectivity (NA) are more likely to report stress symptoms (Spector and O'Connell 1994; Moyle 1995; Cassar and Tattersall 1998). Parkes (1990) suggests that NA has a moderating influence on the stress–strain relationship, making high NA individuals more vulnerable to perceived stress, a hypothesis that has found empirical support (Moyle 1995; Cassar and Tattersall 1998). Research has suggested that workers with particular personality traits are more

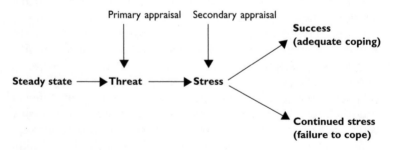

Figure 1.2 The Cooper–Cummings framework model.
Source: adapted from Cartwright and Cooper (1997).

vulnerable to stress: a more 'external' locus of control (Spector 1986; Newton and Keenan 1990; Rees and Cooper 1992) and Type A behaviour pattern (Newton and Keenan 1990). Other personal characteristics, such as age and sex, may also affect vulnerability to stress (Jenkins 1991).

Stressors do not act on a passive individual; he or she is likely to take action to cope with sources of pressure. It is when these coping strategies fail that an individual will experience negative stress outcomes, such as physical or mental ill-health. Proactive, task-focused coping styles, which deal with the problem itself (e.g. improving time management skills to cope with a heavy workload) are likely to be more effective than reactive, emotion-focused coping styles, which aim to mitigate the side-effects (e.g. smoking or drinking alcohol to reduce feelings of anxiety or depression). Koeske et al. (1993) differentiate between two types of coping: control coping (e.g. 'took things a day at a time, one step at a time'; 'considered several alternatives for handling the problem'; 'tried to find out more about the problem') and avoidance coping (e.g. 'avoided being with people in general'; 'kept feelings to myself'; 'drinking more'). In a longitudinal study looking at newly appointed case managers (dealing with challenging patients), they found that control coping had a significant buffering effect over time against the negative consequences of stress; the exclusive use of avoidance coping strategies, in the place of control coping, had detrimental effects. The coping strategies that individuals adopt will depend on a variety of factors including personality, experience and training, for example, Koeske et al. (1993) found that avoidant copers tended to demonstrate a more external locus of control (LOC). Hurrell and Murphy (1991) argue that individuals with an internal LOC suffer from fewer stress symptoms, as they are more likely to define stressors as controllable and take proactive steps to cope with them; however, in work settings where some stressors, such as workload or work pace, are beyond the control of the individual worker, extreme 'internals' may fare no better than moderate or extreme externals. In the latter case, 'emotion-focused' coping strategies may be most effective in reducing distress. Thus, there will be differential effects for some moderators, such as personality and coping mechanisms, depending on the work environment.

Control in the workplace is of particular importance, if individuals are expected to cope successfully with challenging work environments. For example, Cooper et al. (1999) found that anaesthetists felt a lack of control and autonomy at work that had significant negative effects on their well-being. Although individuals can be taught to use proactive coping strategies, the work environment must allow workers a degree of autonomy and decision latitude in order to make use of such coping mechanisms. More recent investigations using Karasek's (1979) measure of job decision latitude and other measures of work control have demonstrated that high levels of control are directly related to a range of positive health and work-related outcomes; for example, decreased anxiety and depression (e.g. Mullarkey *et al.* 1997), life satisfaction (e.g. Fletcher and Jones 1993) and job performance (e.g. Greenberger *et al.* 1989).

Strain

The individual's response to stressors may be manifest as psychological, physical or behavioural symptoms. There are differences in the type of symptoms experienced by an individual in response to exposure to different stressors (Cooper *et al.* 1989), for example, a heavy workload might cause psychological effects in one person, making them anxious, while another might experience headaches. The research evidence supporting the negative effects of stress on individual health is substantive and well documented (Cooper and Cartwright 1994; Cooper 1996). Research reviews indicate that psychological strains, such as anxiety and depression, are strong correlates of work-related stressors (Jackson and Schuler 1985; Jex and Beehr 1991; Kahn and Byosiere 1992). While these may be temporary conditions, experience of one strain can increase vulnerability to other types of strain, e.g. the long-term effects of job dissatisfaction may be physical ill-health and poor psychological well-being. There is substantial evidence to link stress with a number of physical illnesses and disease, particularly high blood pressure and heart attacks (Cooper 1996), but also cancer (Cooper and Watson 1991), irritable bowel syndrome and skin problems, such as eczema (Quick and Quick 1984). Much of the stress literature focuses on health-related outcomes of stress, while behavioural responses to stress, including job performance, turnover, absenteeism, use of alcohol, smoking, substance use and destructive behaviours, are the least studied of all forms of strain, despite their importance to organisations (Cooper *et al.* 2001). The impact of occupational stress on employee-related outcomes is discussed in more detail in Chapter 2.

Risk management of stress

Risk management is a process with which many organisations are
familiar, though mainly in the context of assessing physical hazards
for their impact on the health and safety of employees. The favoured
strategy for assessing all risks to employees' safety and health is risk
management (European Commission (EC) 1996). Some work on the
risk assessment of psychosocial hazards (Cox and Griffiths 1996;
Cox *et al.* 2000) has focused on identifying risk factors related to
employee health. However, psychosocial hazards not only represent
a threat to employees' health, but also influence accident causation
and occupational injuries. Any risk assessment programme aimed at
managing stress must be part of a wider policy on health and safety,
which includes reference to risk factors related both to health and
safety outcomes. The wider implications of psychosocial hazards
have been acknowledged by NIOSH (1996), which states that:
'psychosocial factors . . . have long been recognized as risk factors
for job stress and psychological strain. But recent studies suggest
that work organization may have a broad influence on worker
safety and health and may contribute to occupational injury'.

The Health and Safety Executive (1997) in the United Kingdom
produce advice on the development of a successful health and safety
management system, which includes a systematic approach to
policy, putting policy into practice, planning (including risk
assessment), measuring performance (using active and reactive
measures) and auditing and reviewing performance. The guide to
risk assessment identifies a general model (Health and Safety
Executive 1997), which is based on the same principles as models
used in the United States:

- identification of hazards
- assessment of the associated risks
- design of reasonably practicable control strategies
- implementation of control strategies
- monitoring and evaluation of effectiveness of control strategies
- feedback and reassessment of risk
- review of information needs and training needs of employees.

It has been noted by reviewers of the stress literature that a
systematic risk assessment (identifying risk factors and risk groups)
is often lacking in the practice of stress prevention (Kahn and

Byosiere 1992; Kompier *et al.* 1998). Effective stress management should form part of a broader risk management process that involves, first, hazard identification and assessment; second, risk evaluation (assessment of likely risk factors and risk groups); third, risk reduction (development of a package of risk control measures, to include stress management).

Any risk management methodology aimed at assessing and controlling the risk posed by occupational stress, must take into account the nature and effects of stress. First, stress is subjective, research has identified sources of pressure, but these only lead to negative outcomes if they are 'negatively perceived'; second, the experience of stress is affected by a variety of individual factors, including age, sex, personality and ways of coping; and third, different stressors are more salient in different environments, and different stressors lead to different negative outcomes, requiring a tailored rather than a prescriptive approach to risk reduction.

The structure of the book

Chapters 2–5 provide background information and a research-based rationale for the risk management programme described and illustrated in the later chapters (6–9).

Chapter 2 describes the negative impact of stress at both an individual and organisational level, focusing on the behavioural outcomes that are often neglected by researchers, despite their practical importance to organisations. Chapters 3 and 4 review the environmental and psychological factors influencing occupational safety; these chapters provide an understanding of why accidents occur, and highlight possible ways of reducing them. Chapter 5 reviews the evidence linking stress to occupational safety and accidents, to develop an understanding not only of accident prevention, but also of improving organisational health through integrated health and safety policies.

The risk management approach to stress is described in Chapter 6, including a review of stress management interventions. Chapter 7 focuses on stress assessment, illustrated by a case study based in a UK county council. The identification and evaluation of risk factors is discussed in Chapter 8, including a case study based in the offshore oil industry. Chapter 9 examines strategies for reducing risk, designing effective interventions and monitoring/reviewing the success of interventions.

Chapter 2

The effects of stress on employee-related outcomes

This chapter reviews research evidence of the effects of occupational stress on employee-related outcomes, including health and well-being, reduced productivity, absenteeism, turnover and work-related accidents. These stress outcomes are of particular relevance due to their practical implications for organisations. However, the behavioural symptoms of stress are studied far less frequently than psychological effects.

Reviews of stress research distinguish between three major categories of strain: physiological, psychological and behavioural (Kahn and Byosiere 1992). A literature review conducted by Cooper *et al.* (2001) revealed that the measurement of physiological strain, such as cardiovascular, biochemical and gastrointestinal symptoms (Fried *et al.* 1984), was relatively rare, with the most common measures being blood pressure and heart rate. Self-report measures, utilising checklists of physical symptoms of health, were most popular, and research suggests that such measures are significantly related to a variety of work stressors, but relationships are relatively small (Jex and Beehr 1991). The type of physiological strain produced by an acute stressor may be quite different from that produced by chronic stressors (Fried *et al.* 1984). Research reviews indicate that psychological strains, such as job dissatisfaction and tension/anxiety, are strong correlates of work-related stressors (Jackson and Schuler 1985; Jex and Beehr 1991; Kahn and Byosiere 1992).

As noted in the previous chapter, the research evidence to support the adverse effects that stress has on individual health is well documented (Cooper and Cartwright 1994; Cooper 1996). These negative effects include physical complaints and illnesses (Cooper and Payne 1988; Cooper and Watson 1991) and reduced mental health, such as nervous debility, tension headaches and mental breakdowns (Cartwright and Cooper 1997; see Table 2.1).

The National Council of Compensation Insurance reports that stress at work now represents 11 per cent of all occupational disease claims, and is increasing at a time when other claims are declining (Earnshaw and Cooper 2001). The US Social Security Administration found that, in the early 1990s, stress or psychological disorders are the third most disabling condition in terms of disability allowances (Cartwright and Cooper 1997). The British Household Panel Survey (1998), which gathered data from 5,000 households, found that health problems, including high blood pressure and chronic headaches, were demonstrated to a significantly higher degree in

Table 2.1 Behavioural and physical symptoms of stress

Behavioural symptoms of stress
Constant irritability with people
Difficulty in making decisions
Loss of sense of humour
Suppressed anger
Difficulty in concentrating
Inability to finish one task before rushing into another
Feeling the target of other people's animosity
Feeling unable to cope
Wanting to cry at the smallest problem
Lack of interest in doing things after returning home from work
Waking up in the morning and feeling tired after an early night
Constant tiredness

Physical symptoms of stress
Lack of appetite
Craving for food when under pressure
Frequent indigestion or heartburn
Constipation or diarrhoea
Insomnia
Tendency to sweat for no good reason
Nervous twitches, nail biting, etc.
Headaches
Cramps and muscle spasms
Nausea
Breathlessness without exertion
Fainting spells
Impotency or frigidity
Eczema

Source: adapted from Cartwright and Cooper (1997).

employees who had worked persistently long hours over a five-year period, compared to those working shorter hours. The evidence also suggested that the health problems in these employees persisted following a reduction in work hours, indicating a long-term and irreversible stress-related effect on employee health.

A causal relationship with heart disease is well established (Cooper 1996). A British Heart Foundation report suggested that heart and circulatory disease accounts for 21 per cent of all male absence and 45 per cent of all premature deaths among the working population aged between 35 and 64 each year, at a cost of £2.5 million in lost productive value to the average UK organisation of 10,000 employees (Cooper 1996). Research studies in Japan have demonstrated that heart problems, such as acute myocardial infarction, may result directly from working conditions, e.g. prolonged work hours (Sokejima and Kagamimori 1998), or indirectly due to poor lifestyle habits, e.g. heavy smoking, inadequate diet or lack of exercise (Maruyama *et al.* 1995).

Jex and Beehr (1991) divide behavioural strain into two categories: *significance to the organisation*, including job performance, turnover and absenteeism, and *significance to the individual*, including use of alcohol, smoking, substance use and destructive behaviours. Kahn and Byosiere (1992) identified work role disruptions (performance levels, mistakes, errors and accidents, substance taking at work), job flight (turnover, absenteeism, early retirement, strikes) and aggressive behaviour at work (vandalism, stealing, rumour-spreading and counterproductive behaviours) as forms of behavioural strain. Although objective measurements of behaviour may be gained through observational techniques, the most common approach is to ask people to describe their behavioural responses. Behavioural symptoms may be associated with employee-related outcomes by a direct relationship (e.g. work overload causes absence from work) or mediated by an affective state (e.g. work overload causes anxiety, which in turn causes absenteeism).

Absenteeism, turnover and productivity

As indicated previously, stress has direct effects on employee health and indirect effects, mediated by poor lifestyle habits, such as heavy drinking and smoking. The cost to industry in terms of lost productivity is enormous. Approximately half of all sickness absence is stress-related in the United States (Elkin and Rosch 1990), the United Kingdom (Sigman 1992) and across Europe (Schabracq *et al.* 1996). Paoli (1997) found that 23 per cent of European workers had missed one or more working days in the previous twelve months due to work-related health problems. Workplace stress was identified as the second most frequently cited reason for being absent from work by the CBI (2000) Absence Survey; however, many of the other categories cited were stress-related as well, e.g. personal problems, poor workplace morale, the impact of long work hours, and so on. The Absence Survey listed the following causes of absence for non-manual employees:

- minor illness
- workplace stress
- serious illness
- home and family responsibilities
- personal problems
- paid sickness absence seen as an entitlement
- poor workplace morale
- impact of long hours
- lack of commitment
- leisure accidents
- unauthorised holidays
- work-related accidents.

The UK Whitehall II study (Marmot *et al.* 1995), a longitudinal study conducted on over 10,000 London-based civil servants, suggested that sickness absence can be used as an indicator of physical, psychological and social functioning in studies of working populations. Sickness absence was strongly related to job satisfaction, such that higher rates were found in employees experiencing low job satisfaction. Such findings may suggest that stressed employees, who experience low job satisfaction, use sickness absence as a means of coping, by temporarily removing themselves from a stressful work environment. However, some studies (e.g. Manning and Osland 1989) have failed to find a relationship between stress and subsequent absence, contradicting the view that work absence is a coping response to stress.

In the previous chapter, the damaging effects on employee health of perceived job insecurity and lack of control at work were highlighted. Evidence suggests that there are business costs for organisations associated with increased absenteeism and sickness. Vahtera *et al.* (1997), in a longitudinal study of Finnish government workers, found that medically certified, long-term (over three days) sickness absence was significantly related to the degree of organisational downsizing. There is further evidence that employees who perceive high job insecurity report reduced organisational commitment and lowered motivation (Worrall and Cooper 1998). These psychological effects have behavioural outcomes, in terms of employees reducing efforts to produce a quality output and more actively seeking opportunities for alternative employment (King 2000). However, in evaluating the impact of job insecurity on employee-related outcomes, it is important to consider the type of employment.

Modern workforces are characterised by an increased number of *contingent* workers, employed in 'any job in which the individual does not have an explicit or implicit contract for long-term employment or one in which minimum hours can vary in a non-systematic way' (Beard and Edwards 1995). Contingent work has been described as characterised by job insecurity, low control (in terms of the nature and length of work assignments) and low predictability (in terms of the nature and duration of employment), all of which are associated with reduced job satisfaction, job involvement, organisational commitment and well-being (Beard and Edwards 1995). However, empirical research indicates that choice of employment arrangement is an important predictor of work-related attitudes. Pearce (1993) found that contingent US engineers did not differ significantly from their permanent co-workers in terms of organisational commitment and willingness to engage in extra tasks. Lee and Johnson (1991) found that voluntary temporary workers had the highest level of organisational commit-ment and job satisfaction compared to involuntary temporaries and all permanent workers. The findings of such studies are supported by Canadian researchers (CARNET 1995; Work Family Directions 1993), who have found that employees who are able to choose their work schedules report less stress, greater overall well-being and enhanced work–family balance. Employees who operated on flexible work arrangements had higher performance ratings com-pared to those who were assigned to work schedules. Thus, there were significant positive effects for both well-being and productivity where workers were allowed to exercise choice over their work arrangements.

Findings from the Second European Survey on working conditions, which included data collected from 15,000 employees across fifteen European countries, indicates that for all types of employment, full-time workers tended to report worse health outcomes compared to part-time workers (Benavides *et al.* 2000). Contingent employees experienced higher levels of job dissatisfaction, fatigue, backache and muscular pains, but reported less absenteeism and stress. These findings are supported by a study of 5,600 contingent workers in Scandinavia (Kivimaeki *et al.* 2001). This study demonstrated that contingent employees had a significantly lower rate of medically certified sickness absence, and better self-rated health, compared to permanent employees. Kivimaeki *et al.* (2001) conclude that these differences relate not only to actual employee health, but also to decisions regarding when to take sick leave and when to attend work while ill.

There are direct costs to industry due to lost working days, but there are also indirect costs associated with the reduced performance of individuals who present themselves for work, but are too sick or distressed to work effectively, resulting in a poor quality product or service and increased vulnerability to errors and work-related accidents. There is evidence to suggest that employees who experience high levels of *presenteeism*, also report high levels of sickness absence (Aronsson *et al.* 2000), suggesting that those who continue to work while sick or distressed experience more symptoms than those who do not. Employees most likely to exhibit high sickness presenteeism are those with upper back/neck pain or fatigue/slightly depressed, those whose job involves the provision of care/welfare services or teaching, where difficulties would be experienced in finding a replacement or stand in, and those on a low monthly income (Aronsson *et al.* 2000).

Work-related accidents

Stress is considered to be responsible for 60–80 per cent of all workplace accidents (Cooper *et al.* 1996), yet there is a lack of research examining accidents as an outcome of occupational stress. The focus of research in the safety literature can be divided into environmental and psychological factors (see Chapters 3 and 4), with much emphasis on managerial and organisational antecedents of accidents. Occupational stress is related to increased accident risk in a variety of working environments. For example, in a study of 778 vets, Trimpop *et al.* (2000) used a questionnaire measure of job stress to gauge the presence of stress in the working environment (e.g. 'I experience permanent stress involving the working atmosphere' and 'I find my work strenuous'); job stress was found to be a significant predictor of work accidents. Similarly, a study by Kirkcaldy *et al.* (1997), using a sample of 2,500 doctors, found that job stress was a major predictor of work-related accidents. However, there is little understanding of the mechanisms by which occupational stress affects accident rates. A review of the existing literature is presented in Chapter 5. Experience of workplace stressors may have direct effects on performance, increasing accident liability, or the effects may be indirect, mediated by employee health and well-being. Exposure to long-term stressors will result in psychological and physical symptoms of ill-health (e.g. depression, dissatisfaction and physical illness), these symptoms will then lead to lower performance and increased accident risk. For example, Houston and Allt (1997), in a study of junior house officers, found that psychological distress was linked to significant medical errors, as well as everyday errors, supporting an association between stress symptoms and human error in an organisational setting. A research model discussed by Cooper and Cartwright (1994) identifies individual symptoms (e.g. depressed mood, raised blood pressure) that lead to mental and physical ill-health, and also organisational symptoms (e.g. high absenteeism, high labour turnover) that lead to frequent and severe accidents. This indicates that stress may also have effects at an organisational level that increase the likelihood of accidents, e.g. high absenteeism may lead to staff shortages increasing workload on remaining personnel, thus making errors more probable.

Stressors

The workplace stressors that have been investigated by researchers in relation to work accidents have focused on intrinsic job characteristics (quantitative workload, work schedules and exposure to risk and hazards), organisational roles (role ambiguity, role conflict and role overload), relationships at work (quality of interpersonal relationships and lack of social support from others in the workplace) and career development (job insecurity), with little attention given to the home–work interface. The safety literature has emphasised the role of organisational structure and climate in the causation of accidents, but few researchers have examined these variables in the context of their potential to act as sources of strain (these issues are explored further in Chapter 3).

A number of intrinsic job characteristics have been identified as sources of strain: quantitative overload (the amount of work required and time frame in which the work must be completed; a major source of strain is having to work under time pressure to meet deadlines); qualitative overload (where the individual does not have the opportunity to exercise skills or develop potential ability); work hours (number of hours worked and work schedules, e.g. shift-work); new technology; and exposure to risk and hazards. In terms of work accidents, perceived time pressure and work demands have been investigated, but demonstrate mixed results. Work demands may have direct effects on accident risk, as workers who perceive they are under pressure to increase production may deviate from safety rules that impede their progress, or perform tasks with less care, increasing the likelihood of errors. Work pace (Zohar 1980; M. D. Cooper and Phillips 1994) and conflicts between safety and production (Diaz and Cabrera 1997; Mearns *et al.* 1998) have both emerged as significant factors in the safety literature.

Greiner *et al.* (1998) used observational job analysis to measure stress factors for 308 transit operators performing driving tasks. The study found that two stressors were significantly related to work accidents: time pressure and 'time binding' (autonomy over time management). The risk of work accidents was significantly increased for high time pressure operators and for the medium time-binding group. The findings suggested that changes to the design of the job, which reduce the time pressure to meet deadlines and increased control over the timing of tasks, such as guaranteed rest breaks and flexible timing, would help to reduce accidents. However, Gillen *et al.* (2002) found that perceived job demands (measured using the Job Content Questionnaire) were significantly related to injury severity among construction workers who had suffered falls (when confounding variables were controlled), such that higher job demands were associated with *less* severe injuries. An important variable to consider, in addition to the level of work demands, is the degree of autonomy or control the employee is able to exercise over the work environment. In Karasek's (1979) demands-control model, strain occurs when high job demands are combined with low control, but not when control is high. Thus, in the study conducted by Greiner *et al.* (1998), time binding (autonomy over time management) emerges as a significant variable, in addition to work demands. Although Gillen *et al.* (2002) found the interaction between job demands and decision latitude was not significant, the authors note that: 'although most reported high psychological job demands, they also reported a high degree of decision latitude' (Gillen *et al.* 2002: 46). A number of studies support a relationship between autonomy and work accidents (Harrell 1990) and reported work injuries (Hemingway and Smith 1999), indicating that greater job autonomy is associated with fewer accidents and injuries. Parker *et al.* (2001) found a significant relationship between job autonomy and safe working. This relationship was fully mediated by organisational commitment, indicating that the level of perceived control affects the degree to which employees feel committed to the organisation, which in turn leads to more positive safety behaviour.

Considerable research has been conducted on the effects of work schedules, particularly shift work, on workers' job performance, psychological well-being and work attitudes (Monk *et al.* 1996). This literature indicates a number of problems associated with shift work, including reduced physical and psychological well-being (Monk *et al.* 1996). There is evidence to suggest performance deficits with implications for increased accident risk. For example, Leonard *et al.* (1998) assessed the effects of working a 32-hour on-call shift on junior hospital doctors; the results showed adverse effects on psychological well-being, but moreover, significant detrimental effects on the doctors' alertness and concentration when conducting simple tasks.

Sutherland and Cooper (1991) suggest that perceptions of safety act as a stressor in hazardous working environments, and also that the experience of an accident leads workers to perceive the environment to be more stressful. There is some evidence to support this view. Morrow and Crum (1998) found that perceived dangerousness was a significant predictor of job stress (controlling for objective risk factors, including prior injury and tenure) in US railroad employees. Previously injured offshore workers have been found to feel less safe and experience more job stress (Rundmo 1995). However, in hazardous work environments, it has been suggested that the continued emphasis on the need for safety may be a greater source of strain than the hazards themselves (Cooper *et al.* 2001). Indeed, there is evidence to suggest that intrinsic job hazards in high risk jobs, such as police officers, cause less psychological distress than other stressors, such as organisational climate and structure (Hart *et al.* 1995). McClain (1995) found that while lower perceived safety risk was positively related to satisfaction with workplace conditions, it was unrelated to job stress among fire-fighters and emergency medical technicians. However, greater perceived risk was a significant predictor of greater distraction from task accomplishment, indicating that perceptions of risk may act as distractions for workers, increasing their accident vulnerability.

The 'organisational roles' taken by individuals as part of their jobs can give rise to role-related strain: role ambiguity (unpredictable consequences of one's role performance); role conflict (incompatible demands, within a single role, or between multiple roles); role overload (excessive demands on the individual's time, uncertainty about ability to perform roles effectively); and responsibility (e.g. for other people's safety). There is some evidence to support the relationship between role-related stressors and occupational injuries. Hemingway and Smith (1999) found that workload, role conflict and role ambiguity were significantly related to work-related injuries for 252 Canadian nurses. The authors suggested that lack of job clarity may have a direct effect on injuries as this leads to the individual operating in unfamiliar situations, increasing the likelihood of accidents. Iverson and Erwin (1997), in a sample of 362 Australian blue-collar manufacturing workers, failed to find relationships between workload, role ambiguity or role conflict and occupational injuries that reached significance. However, they did find that employees undertaking more routinised jobs sustained fewer injuries. Iverson and Erwin (1997) suggest that employees undertaking routinised jobs are assigned less responsibility, which decreases their probability of an accident, a finding which is supported by other studies on accidents among blue-collar workers (Hansen 1989; Harrell 1990).

There is consistent evidence to suggest that the quality of 'interpersonal relationships' and 'communication' have a significant association with work accidents. Trimpop *et al.* (2000) found that 'working climate' (communication and relationships with staff) was significantly related to work accidents. Parker *et al.* (2001) conducted a longitudinal study of 161 manufacturing employees' self-reported safe working practices; they found that communication quality had a significant positive relationship with safe working (after prior level of this variable was controlled for). A number of studies have investigated the role of social support from co-workers and supervisors in relation to safety, supporting an association with decreases in accidents (Sherry 1991; Iverson and Erwin 1997). While a lack of social support may act as a source of strain (stressor) for employees (e.g. an unsupportive supervisor can contribute to feelings of job pressure), there is also evidence to suggest that social support acts as a moderator (buffer) in the stress–strain relationship (see discussion later).

Although there has been no empirical work on 'career development' as a stressor, in terms of the effects of promotion and career advancement, a study by Probst and Brubaker (2001) examined the effects of job insecurity (the threat of unemployment) on employee safety outcomes. The study found that job security is significantly related to safety knowledge, safety motivation and reported compliance with safety policies. Injuries and accidents were predicted by safety motivation, and to a lesser degree, by safety knowledge and compliance. The authors noted that 'employees operating under conditions of job insecurity choose to ignore critical safety policies and "cut corners" to maintain or increase their production numbers in an effort to retain their job' (Probst and Brubaker 2001: 19). The relationship between job insecurity and safety motivation was partially mediated by production demands, suggesting that employees who feel more insecure, perceive a greater emphasis on production, which leads to lowered motivation to attend to safety issues. Clarke (2003) discusses the safety implications of an increasingly contingent workforce, particularly noting the difficulties of integrating employees with differing employment arrangements into a shared safety culture.

The empirical work reviewed suggests that stressors at work contribute significantly to workplace accidents. However, there is also limited evidence to support a relationship between job stress and work-related accidents, such as car accidents. In British drivers, Gulian et al. (1989) found that driver stress was associated with reports of work stressors, such as worries about redundancy and retirement. The authors suggest that work demands may influence the driver's general attitude and reactions towards driving. However, these results were not repeated in a sample of Japanese drivers (Matthews et al. 1999), where relatively small relationships were found between occupational stressors, such as work demands, and driver stress. Trimpop et al. (2000) found that job stress was significantly correlated with work accidents, but not with car accidents, in a sample of veterinary surgeons.

Social support

Social support is important as it is thought to *buffer* job stress, that is, individuals who have access to social support are protected from psychological strain (House 1981; Kirmeyer and Dougherty 1988). However, reviews of the literature suggest that there is only weak support for the stress buffering effects of social support on psychological strain (Cooper *et al.* 2001). There is some evidence that buffering effects may be 'washed out' in the presence of chronic (ongoing) stressors (Lepore *et al.* 1991) or even have a 'reverse buffering effect', heightening rather than mitigating psychological strain (Kaufmann and Beehr 1986). In an organisational setting, social support is often provided by immediate colleagues and first-line supervisors; supervisory support is defined as the 'degree of consideration expressed by the immediate supervisor for the sub-ordinates' (Michaels and Spector 1982) and co-worker support as the 'degree of consideration expressed by co-workers' (Blau 1960). Schaubroeck and Fink (1998) found that significant demands–control–support interactions were found more consistently for supervisory support than for support from co-workers, such that high support ameliorates the effects of high strain (low control, high demand) jobs. However, three-way interactions typically account for a small proportion of the variance, 1–3 per cent (Parkes *et al.* 1994). House (1981) differentiates between four kinds of social support:

- *Instrumental support*: giving direct help, often of a practical nature;
- *Emotional support*: showing interest in, understanding of, caring for and sympathy with a person's difficulties;
- *Informational support*: giving the person information that may help him or her deal with problems;
- *Appraisal support*: providing feedback about the person's functioning that may enhance his or her self-esteem.

Research into the effects of social support on stressor–strain relationships has focused on instrumental and emotional support. In terms of accident reduction, social support could take an *informational* role, by providing information to employees on how to deal with safety-related problems, having a direct effect on employee behaviour. It could also have a buffering effect, reducing the psychological strain associated with workplace stressors, by providing instrumental (by helping individuals attend to the problem) and emotional support (by modifying their perception that the stressor is damaging their well-being). Buffering employees against psychological strain, particularly over time, would help to ameliorate the adverse effects on job performance associated with mental and physical ill-health. However, as noted earlier, such effects may be diminished in the longer term.

Iverson and Erwin (1997) examined supervisory and co-worker support in relation to the occupational injuries experienced by Australian manufacturing workers, where the social support variables were operationalised by a modification of the scale by House (1981). The results found that supervisory and co-worker support had a significant negative relationship with occupational injuries, such that greater support was associated with fewer injuries. In this setting, the relationship was thought to stem from supervisors and co-workers providing greater levels of task and informational assistance to employees in carrying out their jobs, that is, increased level of informational support. Similar findings were reported by Hemingway and Smith (1999). This study, looking at occupational injuries among nurses, included supervisor support as an element of organisational climate (subscale of work environment scale: Moos and Insel 1974). Supervisor support had significant negative correlations with unreported injuries ($r = -0.17$, $p<0.05$) and near injuries ($r = -0.15$, $p<0.05$), but not reported injuries. Significant correlations were also found with peer cohesion for reported injuries and near injuries, indicating that close relationships with colleagues was associated with fewer injuries. Gillen *et al.* (2002) used the Job Content Questionnaire to measure decision latitude, psychological demands and social support (supervisor support and co-worker support) in a sample of construction workers. This study found no significant correlations between psychological job demands, decision latitude or social support with injury severity, however, supervisor support approached significance ($r = 0.120, p = 0.056$). In a longitudinal study of manufacturing workers, Parker *et al.* (2001) found that supportive supervision had a lagged positive effect on safe working eighteen months later. Therefore, there is consistent evidence of a significant relationship between social support, particularly from supervisors, and occupational injuries/safe working, suggesting that social support encourages safer working and reduces the number of occupational injuries experienced by workers.

Further research has examined the influence of 'managers' concern' for the general well-being of employees, related to the element of *individualised consideration* (leader shows interest in the personal and professional development of subordinates) (Bass 1985). A supervisor whose leadership style is characterised by individualised consideration would be more likely to demonstrate concern for subordinates' welfare, including emotional support. Zohar (2002a) argues that the leader's concern for members' welfare influences safety behaviour; supervisory response to safety is an interactive function of concern for members' welfare and the safety priorities assigned by senior management. Greater concern for subordinates' welfare is based on closer individualised relationships, which promotes safety-related supervisory practices and, in turn affects workers' safety behaviour. Hofmann and Morgeson (1999) found that high perceived organisational support (POS) was predictive of safety communication (which in turn had an indirect effect on accidents via safety commitment). Thompson *et al.* (1998) examined supervisor support for safety separately from management support; they found that these two variables mediated different relationships, supervisor support mediated the relationship between supervisor fairness and safety compliance, while management support mediated the relationship between organisational politics and safety conditions. A significant positive relationship between supportive leadership and safety communication, with a lagged effect on safety-compliance behaviour eighteen months later, was reported by Parker *et al.* (2001). This research indicates that supportive supervisors build more positive relationships with their subordinates, encouraging more open, informal communications, which in turn, leads to higher levels of safety commitment and compliance among workers.

Other studies have employed measures reflecting social support that have a more specific emphasis on safety. The instrument employed by Oliver *et al.* (2002) gauges 'safety support and behaviour', based on measures developed by Melia *et al.* (1992). 'Supervisory support' reflects the supervisors' attitude towards safety, positive or negative contingencies that the supervisor gives and supervisors' safety behaviour. Tomas *et al.* (1999) report significant positive relationships between workers' safe behaviour and both supervisory response and co-workers' response. Social support (measured by supervisory support and co-worker support) included by Oliver *et al.* (2002) as 'organisational involvement' has a significant direct effect on accidents, but also significant indirect effects, mediated by general health and safe behaviour. These findings support the suggestion earlier that social support may reduce accidents by two means, directly by facilitating safe behaviour, and indirectly by buffering the employee from psychological strain, protecting mental well-being.

The accident causation model developed by Oliver *et al.* (2002) includes direct effects of 'organisational involvement' (supervisor's response, co-worker's response, safety management) and 'the physical work environment' (environmental conditions, noise, workload, hazards) on work accidents. There are also significant paths in the model that support indirect effects, mediated by general health (anxiety checklist, GHQ (General Health Questionnaire) anxiety, GHQ depression). The mediating role of general health supports the proposal by Cox and Cox (1993) that stress processes mediate the effects of both organisational and physical hazards on the individual. Further research has supported an association between health promotion and a lower injury rate (Mearns *et al.* 2003; Shannon *et al.* 1997). This would suggest that better employee health and well-being may act to increase resistance to stress, which in turn reduces accident liability; while, on the other hand, employees suffering psychological distress, such as anxiety and depression, are more prone to errors and accidents. A further effect will result from companies that introduce health promotion programmes as this will increase workers' perceptions that the company is concerned with their well-being.

Job satisfaction

There is evidence to suggest that job satisfaction is significantly lower for employees who have experienced a job-related accident (Holcom *et al.* 1993; Lee 1998). In cross-sectional research, it is possible that this relationship reflects a lowering of job satisfaction as a result of experiencing an accident, as well as a causal link between job dissatisfaction and accident involvement.

In support of a causal relationship between job dissatisfaction and work accidents, low morale and negative work attitudes are associated with attentional deficits and skill-based errors (Edkins and Pollock 1997) and significantly predictive of future errors (Van der Flier and Schoonman 1988). Probst and Brubaker (2001) found that job security perceptions are strongly related to job satisfaction, which in turn is an important predictor of safety motivation and knowledge (in both cross-sectional and longitudinal analyses), suggesting that job satisfaction does have a significant impact on workers' safety behaviour. Job satisfaction is also related to percep-tions of risk. In hazardous work environments, greater perceived risk is associated with low job satisfaction (Fleming *et al.* 1998) and satisfaction with both workplace conditions and with work in general (McClain 1995). These findings would suggest that job satisfaction is linked to enhanced safe working, while job dissatis-faction is associated with lowered job performance and increased accident liability.

There is also support for the hypothesis that the experience of an accident results in lowered job satisfaction. Barling *et al.* (2003), using a sample of 9,908 Australian employees across eight different occupations, found that workplace accidents result in a perceived lack of influence and a distrust of management, which both in turn predict job dissatisfaction.

Summary

This chapter has overviewed the effects of stress in organisational settings, with particular emphasis on behavioural outcomes, such as absenteeism, productivity and work accidents. There has been little emphasis on the relationship between stress and work accidents, but the evidence suggests that job stress affects work accidents by a number of different mechanisms. The existing literature focusing on the causes of work accidents is reviewed in the following chapters. Chapter 3 focuses on environmental and organisational factors, while Chapter 4 overviews individual, psychological influences.

Chapter 3

Environmental factors
and occupational safety

In this chapter, a general overview of the influence of organisational, social and cultural factors on occupational safety is provided. Reason (1993) suggests that there are three overlapping ages of safety concerns: the *technical age*, where the emphasis was on operational and engineering solutions to hazards; the *human error age*, which focused upon the human contribution to accidents, particularly the operators at the 'sharp end' of organisations; and, most recently, the *sociotechnical age*, which recognises that accidents emerge as complex interactions between the technical and the human aspects of systems. The 'human error' age reflected research into accidents occurring from the 1930s through to the 1980s, where a growing body of evidence suggested that human factors were a major contributory factor in accident involvement. However, much emphasis was placed on the human contribution at the level of the individual operator, who was present at the scene of the accident. The growth in popularity of systems theory within management science, with landmark publications, such as Senge (1990), saw its wider application, including to organisational safety. A number of articles were published in the 1990s emphasising the need to take a systems approach to organisational accidents (e.g. Cox 1994; Reason 1995). In this theoretical perspective, put very simply, the 'system' comprises a number of elements and the relationships between those elements. The system is characterised by feedback mechanisms, whereby the behaviour of one element influences the behaviour of other elements. Open systems have permeable boundaries enabling exchanges with the external environment. This perspective extends the scope of factors that may potentially contribute to accidents to all the elements within the system (e.g. operators, supervisors, managers), and the relationships between elements (e.g. ergonomic fit between the operator and the working environment). Case study evidence illustrates the complex interactions and multiple factors that lead to organisational accidents (e.g. Turner 1978; Reason 1990; Toft and Reynolds 1994).

Organisational accidents

Turner (1978) used a number of accident case studies, such as the Aberfan coal-tip slide, which devastated a Welsh village in 1966, to develop a sociotechnical theory of accident causation. He argued that 'it is better to think of the problem of understanding disasters as a "sociotechnical" problem with social organisation and technical processes interacting to produce the phenomena to be studied'. Turner's model of accident causation includes a number of sequential stages through which the accident develops (see Box 3.1). The crucial stage is the 'incubation period' where there is an 'accumulation of an unnoticed set of events which are at odds with the accepted beliefs about hazards and the norms for their avoidance'. The accident sequence begins with notionally normal starting points, but an interacting set of failures develop over time, increasing the organisation's vulnerability to a hazard, the potency of which has been underestimated by the organisation. Within this model, the time frame of an organisational accident can span months, years, even decades, and includes the contribution of individuals far removed from accident onset in both time and space.

Reason (1993: 8) suggests that 'most accidents have their origins within the managerial and organisational spheres'. This is illustrated in Reason's (1990) accident case studies, including the sinking of the *Herald of Free Enterprise* at Zeebrugge (1987) and nuclear disaster at Chernobyl (1988), most of which are based on information gathered through comprehensive official inquiries. Reason argues that accidents occur due to the development of 'latent failures', both organisational and technical, which lead to individual unsafe acts (slips, lapses, mistakes and violations) (see Figure 3.1). The model matches organisational failures with production elements in organisations (high-level decision-makers; line management; workforce; productive activities; defences). Significantly, Reason contrasts delayed-action *latent failures*, which have no immediate negative consequences, but which are found mainly at higher organisational levels, to the slips, lapses and mistakes of individuals, or *active failures*, found mainly at the operational end of the business. Senior

Box 3.1 Turner's (1978) model of accident causation

Stage I: notionally normal starting points
Initially culturally accepted beliefs about the world and its hazards; associated precautionary norms set out in laws, codes of practice, mores and folkways.

Stage II: the incubation period
The accumulation of an unnoticed set of events which are at odds with the accepted beliefs about hazards and the norms for their avoidance.

Stage III: precipitating event
A triggering event forces itself to attention and transforms the general perceptions of Stage II.

Stage IV: onset
The immediate consequence of the collapse of cultural precautions becomes apparent.

Stage V: rescue and salvage – first stage adjustment
The immediate post-collapse situation is recognised in *ad-hoc* adjustments, which permit the work of rescue and salvage to be started.

Stage VI: full cultural readjustment
An inquiry or assessment is carried out and beliefs and precautionary norms are adjusted to fit the newly gained understanding of the world.

managers have the greatest opportunity to contribute to accidents, as the higher the individual's position in the organisation, the greater their potential for latent failures. Fallible decisions are translated into line management deficiencies, creating the preconditions for unsafe acts at an operational level (a workforce lacking training, motivation or the appropriate equipment and technology to do their jobs well). The actions of individuals present at accident onset are active failures. These failures may act to *trigger* an accident, rather than *cause* an accident, as they activate the adverse effects of latent failures, which were lying dormant within the system.

Safety systems based on Reason's model have been developed,

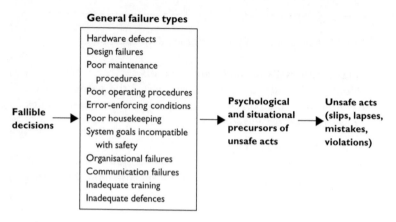

General failure types

Fallible decisions →

Hardware defects
Design failures
Poor maintenance
    procedures
Poor operating procedures
Error-enforcing conditions
Poor housekeeping
System goals incompatible
    with safety
Organisational failures
Communication failures
Inadequate training
Inadequate defences

→ Psychological and situational precursors of unsafe acts

→ Unsafe acts (slips, lapses, mistakes, violations)

Figure 3.1 Reason's accident causation model.

Source: adapted from Reason (1993).

initially for the oil industry and the UK railways (described in Reason 1993, 1995), which focus on the proactive identification and remediation of organisational factors, and later applications within the airline industry and medicine (Reason 1997, 1998). Australian railways have also adopted a system based on these ideas (Edkins and Pollock 1997).

Organisation and management

Despite the general tendency for early accident research to focus on the role of technical failures and human error, there were some notable exceptions. A number of empirical studies focused on the organisational and social factors which differentiate between high and low accident departments or companies (e.g. Keenan *et al.* 1951; Cohen *et al.* 1975) and which determine successful safety programmes (Cohen 1977; Smith *et al.* 1978). These studies identified the following factors as important: top management personally involved on a routine basis; safety is integral and given high priority in meetings; high status of safety officers; emphasis on safety training; open communication links between workers and managers; environmental control and good housekeeping; stable workforce (good industrial relations and personnel procedures).

Based on case study analysis, Reason (1993, 1995) identifies eleven categories of latent failure:

- hardware defects
- design failures
- poor maintenance procedures
- poor operating procedures
- error-enforcing conditions
- poor housekeeping
- system goals incompatible with safety
- organisational failures
- communication failures
- inadequate training
- inadequate defences.

Reason suggests that a profile can be developed to reflect the organisation's weaknesses within these categories. The most common categories are communication and organisational failures.

Although Reason's organisational factors are based on case study analysis, there is some confirmation of these factors in empirical research. In a review of ten studies, Shannon *et al.* (1997) found that a number of organisational factors were consistently related to lower injury rates, based within six categories. Factors within the 'Management style and culture' and 'Organisational philosophy on occupational health and safety (OHS)' were most common:

Management style and culture
- empowerment of the workforce
- long-term commitment of workforce encouraged
- good relations between management and workers.

Organisational philosophy on OHS
- delegation of safety activities
- active role of top management
- safety audits conducted
- evaluation of occupational safety hazards
- unsafe worker behaviours monitored
- duration of safety training of workers
- safety training on a regular basis
- employee health screening.

Shannon *et al.* (1997: 215) note that the majority of significant factors seem to reflect 'a genuine concern by management for its workforce. It is unlikely that this can be acquired simply by "tinkering" with policies and practices'. Other significant factors included low turnover, seniority of the workforce, good house-keeping and safety controls on machinery.

Safety management practices

Safety management relates to the actual practices, roles and functions associated with remaining safe (Kirwan 1998). Recent studies have examined the extent to which specific management practices are related to accidents (Mearns *et al.* 2003; Vredenburgh 2002).

Vredenburgh (2002) examined six management practices (management commitment, rewards, communication and feedback, selection, training and participation) as predictors of injury rate. Overall, the management practices were significantly predictive of hospital injury rates, accounting for approximately 17 per cent of the variation in injuries, with 'hiring practices' the only significant predictor. However, factor analysis revealed that the items measuring the six management practices did not correspond as intended, instead six factor scales were produced. Two of these were significantly predictive of injuries: Factor 1 (reactive practices) and Factor 2 (proactive practices). Factor 2 (selection and training items) was a significant predictor, while Factor 1 (analysis of near-misses, enforcement of safety procedures) acted as a suppressor. This suggests that hospitals with low injury rates perform both proactive and reactive management practices, while those with high injury rates are primarily concerned with reactive responses. Vredenburgh (2002) suggests that front-end hiring and training of employees is most effective in reducing injuries, e.g. interviewers could use behavioural based interviewing techniques to assess potential employees' safety record.

Mearns *et al.* (2003) looked at safety management practices (policies for health and safety, organising for health and safety, management commitment, involvement, health promotion and surveillance, health and safety auditing) and their association with lower accident rates. Three general areas were identified:

- *genuine and consistent management commitment to safety*: prioritisation of safety over production; maintaining a high profile for safety in meetings; personal attendance of managers at safety meetings and in walkabouts; face-to-face meetings with employees that feature safety as a topic; job descriptions that include safety contracts;

- *communications about safety issues*: pervasive channels of formal and informal communication and regular communication between management, supervisors and the workforce;
- *involvement of employees*: empowerment, delegation of responsibility for safety, and encouraging commitment to the organisation.

Mearns *et al.* (2003) found that all safety management practices were associated with lower proportions of individuals reporting an accident and with lower official accident reports. Different indicators of accident rate demonstrated slightly different results, thus fewer lost time injuries were significantly related to health promotion and surveillance and health and safety auditing (inspection targets, corrective actions taken, health and safety goal-setting) and lower official accident rates were significantly related to health and safety auditing. The results highlighted the relationship between health promotion and lower injury rate (a finding supported by Shannon *et al.* 1997).

These studies indicate the importance of both reactive monitoring of organisational safety by senior managers (e.g. through health and safety auditing), but also proactive measures to ensure safety. Indeed, Vredenburgh (2002) suggests that it is the combination of these two approaches to organisational safety that is related to injury rates. Mearns *et al.* (2003) summarise the key organisational factors as management commitment to safety, communication between managers and the workforce, and the involvement of employees. Management practices related to these factors, such as senior managers attending safety meetings, safety training and empowerment of the workforce are consistently associated with lower injury rates.

Safety culture

The accidents at Three Mile Island (United States) in 1979 and, later, at Chernobyl (Russia) in 1986, focused global attention on the issue of nuclear safety. Government attempts to quell the fears of the Western world about the safety of nuclear installations emphasised that such an incident could not happen in the West because of the superior 'safety culture'. Giving a high priority to safety issues was defined by the International Atomic Energy Agency (IAEA) as being indicative of a 'safety culture' (IAEA 1986; INSAG (International Nuclear Safety Advisory Group) 1991). The IAEA (1988) defined safety culture as 'that assembly of characteristics and attitudes in organisations and individuals which establishes that, as an overriding priority, nuclear safety issues receive the attention warranted by their significance'. A similar safety alert was felt by the chemical industry in the wake of the disaster at Bhopal (India) in 1984.

Following the Chernobyl accident, a number of other major disasters, which were subject to detailed independent public inquiry in the United Kingdom, revealed the significant role played by organisational and social factors. The term *safety culture* was quoted by several of these inquiry reports as an explanatory concept for the way that a combination of managerial, organisational and social factors caused each of the accidents: Zeebrugge ferry sinking (Sheen 1987); King's Cross underground station fire (Fennell 1988); Clapham Junction rail disaster (Hidden 1989); Piper Alpha offshore platform fire (Cullen 1990). Thus, the idea of safety culture was highlighted for a broader range of organisations, involved in transportation and public safety, as well as the high hazard nuclear and chemical industries. The concept of safety culture drew the attention of government agencies, including the UK Health and Safety Commission (HSC) and the Occupational Health and Safety Administration (OSHA) in the United States, who suggest that companies reduce their accident rate by developing a *positive safety culture* (e.g. HSE 1991). This was defined by the Advisory Committee on the Safety of Nuclear Installations (ACSNI) as 'the product of individual and group values, attitudes, perceptions, competencies, and patterns of behaviour that determine the commitment to, and the style and proficiency of, an organisation's health and safety management' (HSC 1993: 23) and has since been widely used as a working definition of safety culture. A positive safety culture is characterised by 'communications founded on mutual trust, by shared perceptions of the importance of safety and by confidence in the efficacy of preventive measures' (HSC 1993).

Glendon and Stanton (1998) describe the notion of safety culture as arising largely from ideas about the concept of organisational culture. Glendon and colleagues suggest that safety culture should be regarded as 'those aspects of culture that affect safety' (Glendon and McKenna 1995; Waring and Glendon 1998). An examination of the history of the term suggests that safety culture is not directly derived from a broader understanding of organisational culture, but it is fair to suggest that safety culture shares many of the features of organisational culture, despite being theoretically underspecified.

Pidgeon (1991: 135) considers culture to be 'a shared meaning system' and safety culture to be 'the constructed system of meanings through which a given people or group understand the hazards of the world'. Thus, safety culture is essentially a social phenomenon, as its definition depends on individuals' perceptions being shared within a group context; a feature which is reflected in many definitions, for example, Cox and Cox (1991) and HSC (1993) both refer to 'shared perceptions of safety' and M. D. Cooper and Phillips (1994) to 'a collective commitment of care and concern'. Definitions of organisational culture also emphasise its shared or social nature (e.g. Bate 1984; Schein 1985). However, Turner (1991) notes that while safety culture has important social dimensions, it also has a technical aspect, which should not be overlooked; he emphasises the nature of safety culture as sociotechnical, rather than wholly social.

Cox and Cox (1996) and Reason (1997) make a distinction between safety culture as something that an organisation 'is' and something that an organisation 'has'. This distinction has been described as reflecting two broad and contrasting perspectives: the *interpretive* versus the *functionalist* approach (Waring 1996; Waring and Glendon 1998). Cox and Cox (1996) describe safety culture as an 'emergent property' of the organisation as a system; several authors have used the gestaltist phrase 'greater than the sum of its parts' (Cox and Cox 1996; Reason 1997; Lee 1998). These *interpretive* standpoints assume that safety culture is a complex outcome of all people in the organisation (not just senior managers); strategy supports culture (not vice versa); it cannot be trained or sloganised into people; culture change cannot be engineered quickly, but is slow by 'learning' (Waring 1996). The implication of the interpretive view is that culture cannot be considered as a 'simple thing that can be bolted on to an organisation' (Turner *et al.* 1989); safety culture is not easily developed, changed or manipulated, an implication which contrasts with the *functionalist* view which suggests that culture is amenable to management control, as it is essentially an expression of organisational strategy. M. D. Cooper and Phillips (1995) argue that because safety culture is expressed in goal-directed behaviour this allows actions to be formulated that 'shape, change, or manage safety culture', and Reason (1997: 192) that safety culture can be 'socially engineered' by 'identifying and fabricating its essential components and then assembling them into a working whole'. The latter view favours the regulators' approach that companies can change their existing safety culture to one which will result in improved safety performance, while the former view indicates that such a change will be difficult to achieve and cannot be imposed by senior management. The line drawn between an interpretive and a functionalist approach is not always so clear in practical terms, many pragmatic researchers acknowledge the complex and pluralistic nature of safety culture, but employ simpler operationalisations in practice, likewise many companies 'mix and match' their diagnostic and auditing tools to reflect both approaches.

Hopfl (1994) warns that management attempts to impose a 'corporate culture' on employees can conceal discrepancies and gloss over the dysfunctional. The mechanisms used to develop a corporate safety culture may focus on a common rhetoric, under-pinned by the observable artefacts of a 'safety culture' (such as the appropriate methods, manuals, systems and structures), which ensure the standardised behaviour of employees. However, the over-emphasis on the external appearance of safety can lead to employees placing greater stress on consensus of behaviour than the meanings upon which that behaviour is based. Hopfl suggests that a safety culture must imply 'some level of relationship between the corporate culture of an organisation and the culture of the workplace' (1994: 55). Likewise, Reason (1997) implies that while one can identify and develop the essential characteristics of a safety culture through 'social engineering', this is not enough to truly have a safety culture. One can construct the elements of a safety culture, but like Frankenstein's monster, it requires a certain spark to bring it to life.

'Organisational culture' has been described as being 'multi-layered', with three levels commonly distinguished: deepest level (core assumptions); intermediate (beliefs and values); surface manifestations (norms and artefacts) (e.g. Schein 1985). Safety culture has also been described as existing at differing levels, being 'the specific set of norms, beliefs, roles, attitudes and practices within an organisation which is concerned with minimising exposure of employees, managers, customers, suppliers and members of the general public to conditions considered to be dangerous or injurious' (Turner 1991: 241). In reviewing the literature on organisational culture and safety culture, Guldenmund (2000: 251) defines *safety culture* as 'those aspects of the organisational culture which will impact on attitudes and behaviour related to increasing or decreasing risk'. He conceptualises safety culture as having three levels: outer layer (artefacts, e.g. statements, meetings, inspection reports, posters); middle layer (espoused values/attitudes regarding hardware, software, people and risks, e.g. attitudes, policies, procedures, job descriptions); core (basic assumptions regarding the nature of reality and truth, time, space, human nature, human activity and human relationships). Much research has focused on the expression of safety culture at the intermediate level, through the measurement of perceptions and safety attitudes. However, some researchers have emphasised the behavioural expression of safety culture in the work behaviour of employees. Merritt and Helmreich (1996) view safety culture primarily as a frame of reference within which company safety policy and regulations are interpreted; Guest *et al.* (1994: 2) note that it 'will include the way these issues [risk and danger] are viewed and the priority attached to them in determining day-to-day behaviour'. M. D. Cooper and Phillips (1995: 6) venture further, stating that safety culture is 'reflected in the dynamic interrelationships between members' perceptions about and attitudes towards organisational goals; members' day-to-day goal-directed behaviour; and the presence and quality of organisational systems to support goal-directed behaviour'. While reference is often made to values, beliefs and assumptions in definitions, unlike attitudes and behaviours, they are rarely tapped by measures of safety culture.

Pidgeon (1991) discusses the characteristics of a *good safety culture* (as opposed to the failures highlighted by accident analyses said to reveal a poor safety culture). He argues that there are three essential elements of a good safety culture: *norms and rules* for handling hazards (these are explicit or tacit corporate guidelines for defining what is and is not to be regarded as a significant risk); *attitudes* towards safety (individual and collective beliefs about hazards and the importance of safety, together with the motivation to act on those beliefs); *reflexivity* on safety practice (a search for new meanings in the face of uncertainty and ambiguity about risk). Pidgeon elaborates that effective norms and rules are not just about developing prescriptive procedures to deal with foreseeable hazards, but being alert to unforeseen hazards, and monitoring for information from a variety of sources, including 'outsiders' and internal 'whistleblowers'. This openness operates at both an individual and a collective level. The promotion of safety attitudes depends on the propagation of norms and rules for handling hazards throughout the organisation, and for senior managers to hold realistic views about the organisation regarding hazards. Positive safety attitudes need to be developed by all members of the organisation and cannot be imposed by any one group. Finally, Pidgeon suggests that reflexivity can be developed through feedback systems, for example, incident, accident and near-miss reporting, at an industry-wide, as well as an organisational level.

Safety climate

Within the safety literature, the term *safety climate* is used, often interchangeably with safety culture, although this term has a different history and has been studied independently from safety culture. Based on the work of Schneider (1975) on organisational climates, Zohar (1980) followed the suggestion that facet-specific climates should be investigated and developed a measure of 'safety climate'. Zohar took the organisational and social factors identified in previous studies and devised a questionnaire to examine how these factors were *perceived by the workforce. Climate* was defined as 'a summary of molar perceptions that employees share about their work environments . . . a frame of reference for guiding appropriate and adaptive task behaviours' (Zohar 1980: 96). Safety climate scores were expected to correlate with company accident rate, as the climate acts as a frame of reference for behaviours. Further studies have attempted to replicate and develop Zohar's (1980) work in different industries and cultural contexts (Brown and Holmes 1986; Dedobbeleer and Beland 1991; M. D. Cooper and Phillips 1994; Hofmann and Stetzer 1996; Diaz and Cabrera 1997).

The definition of safety climate suggests that it might be regarded as a mediating variable between organisational characteristics and workers' safe/unsafe behaviours. Empirical studies have supported a mediation role for safety climate (Neal *et al.* 2000; Barling *et al.* 2002; Griffin *et al.* 2002; Zohar 2002a). Safety climate has been found to mediate the relationship between organisational climate (Neal *et al.* 2000), leadership style (Zohar 2002a, 2002b) and local leadership (Griffin *et al.* 2002) on measures of safety performance.

A debate has developed over the difference between 'safety culture' and 'safety climate'. Many earlier studies have looked at 'safety climate' as a specific organisational climate, after Zohar (1980), but often later ones (post-1986) are explicitly examining safety attitudes as being indicative of the organisation's safety culture, for example, Cox and Cox (1991: 93), who state that 'safety cultures reflect the attitudes, beliefs, perceptions and values that employees *share* in relation to safety' (original italics). Cox and Cox (1996) reflect on Pidgeon's (1991) definition of a good safety culture as having three elements, norms and rules, safety attitudes and reflexivity, but propose that 'positive attitudes to safety are arguably the most important aspects of a "good" safety culture' (Cox and Cox: 1996: 117). This argument is followed by later researchers, who operationalise safety culture as the safety attitudes of organisational members (predominantly workers) and develop safety attitude questionnaires as indicative of the safety culture (Lee 1998; Cheyne *et al.* 1998). Nevertheless, the waters remain muddied as Lee (1998) talks of assessing the 'safety culture', while Cheyne *et al.* (1998) still refer to the 'safety climate'. The differences between these two concepts has been further debated (Flin 1998; Cox and Flin 1998; Mearns *et al.* 1998), including calls for the discussions within the 'parallel' debate in organisational psychology (e.g. Denison 1996) to enlighten the one in safety science. The real difficulty lies in the atheoretical roots of safety culture: while researchers have conveniently attached the concept to an existing literature on safety climate, operationalising safety culture as 'shared attitudes towards safety', no one has developed an independent theoretical framework and attempted to operationalise safety culture on the basis of such a theory. It has been noted by Kennedy and Kirwan (1995) and Pidgeon (1998) that safety culture is underspecified in theoretical terms. Although a few attempts have been made to develop the theory of safety culture (Guldenmund 2000; Clarke 2000).

A major theme in empirical studies has been defining the dimensions or components of safety climate/safety culture. Clarke (2000) presents an overview of sixteen empirical studies that involved development of the architecture of safety attitudes (see Table 3.1). There is much variation in the number of dimensions; these vary from global measures of safety climate to sixteen distinct components. Clarke (2000) identifies five dominant themes: work task/ work environment; personal involvement and responsibility; management attitudes; safety management system; management actions. Flin *et al.* (2000) reviewed sixteen studies and also identified five factors: management, safety system, risk, work pressure and competence. The authors noted that the most typically assessed

Table 3.1 Summary of sixteen safety climate studies

Study	Industrial sector	Sample (including N)	Instrument	Dimensions	Outcome measures (if any)
Zohar (1980)	Production (metal, food, chemical, textile)	20 workers from each of 16 factories (Israel) (N = 380)	Questionnaire developed for the study (40 items)	Exploratory FA: 8 factors Perceived importance of safety training programmes Perceived management attitudes to safety Perceived effects of safe conduct on promotion Perceived level of risk in the workplace Perceived effects of required workpace on safety Perceived status of safety officer Perceived effects of safe conduct on social status Perceived status of safety committee	Judges' rankings of factories
Brown and Holmes (1986)	Manufacturing and production	Production workers in 10 companies (US) (N = 425)	Zohar's (1980) questionnaire	Confirmatory FA: 3 factors Management concern Management action Level of risk	Accidents: one accident in previous year (N = 200) vs none (N = 225)
Dedobbeleer and Beland (1991)	Construction	Construction workers on 9 sites (US) (N = 272)	Zohar's (1980) questionnaire	WLS method: 2 factors Management commitment to safety Workers' involvement in safety	None
Cooper and Phillips (1994)	Production	Workers in a packaging production plant (UK) (N = 374); same plant 12 months later (N = 187)	Questionnaire based on Zohar (1980) – 50 items (divided into 7 scales)	Second-order FA of 7 scales: 2 factors (same factors found for both samples) Factor 1: direct Perceived level of risk Management attitudes toward safety Effects of workpace Management actions toward safety Importance of safety training	Accidents: 4 groups – none, minor only, major minor only, minor and major

Study	Industry	Sample	Measure	Factors/dimensions	Outcomes
Hofmann and Stetzer (1996)	Chemical	Managers, administrators and workers at a chemical processing plant (US) (N = 204); divided into 21 teams (N = 21)	Dedobeleer and Beland's (1991) questionnaire (9 items)	Factor 2: indirect Social status and promotion Safety officer and committee Importance of safety training Used global measure of safety climate ($r = 0.78$, between two dimensions)	Unsafe behaviours Accidents
Diaz and Cabrera (1997)	Aviation (ground handling, fuel company and airport authority)	Company 1 (N = 78) – managers (10%), supervisors (5%) and handling operators (85%); company 2 (N = 39) – managers (10%) and operators (92%); company 3 (N = 49) – managers (37%), supervisors (24%) and operators (39%) (Spain) (Total N = 166)	Safety climate questionnaire based on Zohar (1980) – 33 items	Exploratory FA: 6 factors Company policies towards safety Emphasis on productivity versus safety Group attitudes towards safety Specific strategies for prevention Safety level perceived in the airport Safety level perceived on the job	Safety level (includes measure of accidents)

Table 3.1 Continued

Study	Industrial sector	Sample (including N)	Instrument	Dimensions	Outcome measures (if any)
Cox and Cox (1991)	Production (industrial gases)	Production workers (Europe: UK, Germany, Belgium, France and Holland) (N = 630)	Questionnaire developed for the study (18 items)	Exploratory FA: 5 factors Personal scepticism Individual responsibility Safeness of the work environment Effectiveness of arrangements for safety Personal immunity	None
Cox et al. (1998)	Manufacturing	Managers (6%), supervisors (5%) and workers (89%) from 13 companies (UK) (N = 3,329)	Cox and Cox (1991) questionnaire	Confirmatory FA: 3 factors Management actions for safety Quality of safety training Personal actions for safety	Appraisal of commitment to safety
Cheyne et al. (1998)	Manufacturing	Managers (6%), supervisors (8%) and workers (75%) from European factories (UK and France) (N = 915)	Questionnaire based on Cox and Cox (1991) and Tomas and Oliver (1995) (30 items)	Confirmatory FA: 5 factors Safety management Individual responsibility Safety standards and goals Personal involvement	Safety activities

Study	Industry	Sample	Measure	Factors/Scales	Outcome
Donald and Canter (1994)	Chemical processing	Workers at 10 chemical processing sites (UK) (total N = 701)	Questionnaire developed for the study	Theoretically derived pre-set scales: Self Workmates Supervisors Managers Safety representatives Satisfaction Knowledge Action Passive safety behaviour Active safety behaviour	Accidents
Alexander et al. (1994)	Offshore oil and gas production	Onshore and offshore employees (UK) (N = 558)	Questionnaire developed for the study (40 items – 4 applicable only to offshore)	Exploratory FA: 6 factors Overt management commitment Personal need for safety Personal appreciation of risk Attributions of blame Conflict and control Supportive environment	Accidents: accident group (N = 64) vs no accident (N = 494)
Mearns et al. (1998)	Offshore oil and gas production	233 supervisors and 479 workers from 10 offshore installations (UK) (N = 722)	Offshore Safety Questionnaire (52 items)	Exploratory FA: 10 factors Speaking up about safety Attitude to violations Supervisor commitment to safety Attitude to rules and regulations OIM commitment to safety Safety regulation Cost versus safety Personal responsibility for safety Safety systems Over-confidence in own safety	Accidents/near-miss: any accident/near-miss during previous 2 years on current installation vs none

Table 3.1 Continued

Study	Industrial sector	Sample (including N)	Instrument	Dimensions	Outcome measures (if any)
Lee (1998)	Nuclear	Employees from BNFL Sellafield site (UK) (N = 5,296)	Questionnaire developed for the study (172 items)	Exploratory FA: 38 factors (reduced to 15 through domain analysis) Confidence in safety procedures Personal caution over risks Perceived level of risk at work Trust in workforce Personal interest in job Contentment with job Satisfaction with work relationships Satisfaction with rewards for good work Personal understanding of safety rules Satisfaction with training Satisfaction with staff suitability Perceived source of safety suggestions Perceived source of safety actions Perceived personal control over safety Satisfaction with design of plant	Accidents: at least one LT accident (3 + days) (N = 684) vs none (N = 4,514)
Niskanen (1994)	Road administration	1,890 workers and 562 supervisors in road maintenance, construction and repair (Finland) (N = 2,452)	Questionnaire developed for the study (25 items – workers; 18 items – supervisors)	Exploratory FA (workers, N = 1,890): 4 factors Attitude towards safety in the organisation Changes in work demands Appreciation of the work Safety as part of productive work Exploratory FA (supervisors, N = 562): 4 factors Changes in job demands Attitude towards safety in the organisation Value of the work Safety as part of productive work	High vs low accident workplaces

| Williamson et al. (1997) | Heavy and light manufacturing; outdoor workers | Workers from 7 workplaces (Australia) (N = 660) | Questionnaire developed for the study (62 items – reduced to 32 items) | Exploratory FA: 5 factors (from reduced set of items)
Personal motivation for safe behaviour
Positive safety practice
Risk justification
Fatalism
Optimism
Further reduction resulted in acceptable global measure of safety climate (17 items) | Had an accident while working: yes, no |
| Coyle et al. (1995) | Clerical and service | Two organisational samples:
N1 = 340 and
N2 = 540
(Australia)
(Total N = 880) | Questionnaire developed for the study (26 items) | Exploratory FA of organisation 1 (N = 340): 6 factors
Maintenance and management issues
Company policy
Accountability
Training and management attitudes
Work environment
Policy/procedures
Personal authority
Exploratory FA of organisation 2 (N = 540): 3 factors
Work environment
Personal authority
Training and enforcement of policy | None |

dimensions of safety climate relate to management (72 per cent of studies), the safety system (67 per cent) and risk (67 per cent).

Williamson *et al.* (1997) note that different approaches to the components of safety climate are partially responsible for the differences in dimensions found by empirical studies. They identify two differing approaches: first, asking workers for their perceptions of actual workplace characteristics (e.g. Zohar 1980); second, asking more general questions about safety (e.g. Cox and Cox 1991). Additionally, many studies lack any theoretical underpinning and construct their measurement tools by selecting items from previous questionnaires, although some studies demonstrate a systematic approach to item generation (Cox and Cox 1991; Donald and Canter 1994).

A review of several empirical studies has provided evidence of a significant relationship between a more positive safety climate and fewer accidents (Clarke 2000). Safety climate scores aggregated across teams were found to correlate significantly with the teams' level of unsafe behaviours and accident rate (Hofmann and Stetzer 1996), and Donald and Canter (1994) found significant correlations with all safety climate scales (except safety representatives) and accidents. Other studies have found significantly more positive safety climate scores for non-accident involved workers. Comparing accident and non-accident groups: Brown and Holmes (1986) found significant differences on all three dimensions; Williamson *et al.* (1997) for two of five dimensions and marginally ($p<0.06$) for the global safety climate scale; Mearns *et al.* (1998) for seven of ten dimensions; and Varonen and Mattila (2000) for two of four dimensions. The majority of empirical studies have supported a relationship between safety climate (or some aspects of it) and safety performance, although a few studies have found no relationship (e.g. Alexander *et al.* 1994). Glendon and Litherland (2001) failed to find a significant relationship between safety climate and safety performance (observed safe and unsafe behaviours).

It should be noted that these findings encompass different levels of analysis: *individual* level (dividing employees within a company into accident versus non-accident groups and comparing individual safety climate scores); *team* level (aggregating climate scores across teams, groups or departments and comparing against group accident rates); and *company* level (high and low accident companies compared on aggregated climate scores). Different levels of analysis can generate differing results, for example, Hofmann and Stetzer (1996) found a negative correlation between climate scores and unsafe behaviours at a team level ($r = -0.66$, $p<0.01$), but a positive correlation at an individual level ($r = 0.34$, $p<0.01$). Another difficulty is the type of outcome measure used, as accidents are rare (particularly at an individual level), alternative measures are employed, e.g. self-reports of incidents/near-misses or safety activities. Thus results may differ, depending on the type of outcome measure used.

Although there are wide variations in the number and content of safety climate dimensions, it is possible to extract the dominant themes common across studies (Clarke 2000; Flin *et al.* 2000). This suggests that similar themes are being reflected in the measures, but that variations in the way that issues are presented in questionnaires may contribute to differences in factor structures. Some reviews (Clarke 2000; Flin *et al.* 2000) agree on a number of primary dimensions of safety climate, including *management commitment* (managers' actions and attitudes regarding safety); *safety management system* (perceptions of/satisfaction with company safety policy and procedures) and *risk* (level of workplace risk and how this is perceived by the workforce). Flin *et al.* (2000) suggest that it may be possible to identify a core set of dimensions of safety climate that represent generic, underlying factors akin to the 'Big Five' of personality. However, a number of empirical studies, which have used similar safety culture measures in different industries, have concluded that the structure of safety attitudes is context-dependent (Coyle *et al.* 1995; Cox *et al.* 1998). The studies overviewed in Table 3.1 demonstrate the diversity of industries and cultures in which safety climate has been measured. Brown and Holmes (1986) failed to replicate Zohar's (1980) factor structure (Israeli production workers) using a US sample of production workers; Dedobbeleer and Beland (1991) failed to replicate Brown and Holmes' (1986) factor structure, using a US sample of construction workers. Thus, differing factor structures were found for different industries (production versus construction) and for different cultures (Israeli versus US). M. D. Cooper and Phillips (1994) argue that sampling across different plants, factories or sites introduces error variance, due to differing subclimates associated with workplaces, which explains the failure to replicate Zohar's original factor structure. Similarly, the five-factor model found by Cox and Cox (1991) was not replicated in later confirmatory analyses (Cox *et al.* 1998;

Cheyne *et al.* 1998). However, Cheyne *et al.* found that the factor structure remained stable across the four plants sampled in the study (one in France and three in the United Kingdom). Janssens *et al.* (1995) also found that the factor structure in their cross-cultural study was stable, but that the strength of the relationships in the structural model differed across countries.

Thus, some degree of stability in factor structure has been supported across plants within the same multinational organisation in different countries (Janssens *et al.* 1995; Cheyne *et al.* 1998) and within the same country across similar industrial sectors (Varonen and Mattila 2000). However, it does seem to be strongly influenced by the type of industry, in that dimensions vary due to the method of questionnaire development that reflect issues pertinent to a particular organisation. Variations in physical hazards, work environment, team-working, prevalence of written rules and regulations, style of management, intensity of supervision and prominence of safety representatives and safety committees, will all be reflected in measures of safety climate. Glendon and Litherland (2001) found differences between job types, but not between districts, on two of six safety climate factors: 'relationships' and 'safety rules'. They hypothesised that the differences were due to varying work environments (i.e. level of supervisor contact and degree of formalisation).

There are common themes that emerge from the literature regarding safety culture and safety climate to indicate that workers' perceptions of management commitment to safety, the adequacy of the safety management system and their own attitudes towards risk and safety, are important for occupational safety. These are discussed in the following sections.

Perceptions of management commitment to safety

One recurring theme within the research is the importance of senior managers' commitment to safety, and moreover, the extent to which that commitment is perceived as genuine by the workforce. Cox *et al.* (1998) suggest that management actions have the greatest significant effect on workers' appraisal of commitment. Management actions for safety comprised the following nine items:

- quality of near-miss reporting*
- quality of preventive and corrective actions for safety*
- focus on preventing accidents rather than blaming workers

- setting a good example on safety*
- encouragement of safety suggestions*
- effectiveness of safety committees
- priority accorded to safety in relation to other management issues*
- saliency of profit motives in relation to safety issues*
- continuity and consistency of safety management practices.*

There is empirical evidence for a relationship between several of these items and safety outcome measures (indicated by an asterisk). Monitoring of workers' unsafe behaviours is consistently related to lower injury rates (Shannon et al. 1997). The importance of both preventive and corrective safety measures is suggested by Vreden-burgh (2002). Janssens et al. (1995) supported a strong relationship between priority given to safety versus production on perceived safety level, and Mearns et al. (2003) found that prioritisation of safety over production was significantly related to lower injury rates. Asfahl (1984) found that US managers' interest and involvement in safety resulted in lowered injury rates, while an emphasis on production is reflected in poor working conditions, tight schedules and unsafe work layouts. Senior management commitment to safety initiatives has been demonstrated as a key to their success (Griffiths 1985). A lack of perceived managerial commitment to safety is reflected in workers' own safety attitudes and behaviour (Clarke 1998a, 1998b). Clarke (1998a) has shown that train drivers' intentions to report safety-related incidents are significantly reduced where managers are perceived to be uninter-ested in reports and reluctant to act upon them. Management support for safety has been shown to mediate the relationship between organisational politics (the extent to which employees perceived they could elevate safety issues to managers) and safety conditions (Witt et al. 1994; Thompson et al. 1998). Witt et al. (1994) also found that policy–practice inconsistency had an indirect effect on safety conditions mediated by management support. There is a close relationship between management actions and manage-ment attitudes (especially given a lack of contact with managers, workers' perceptions of commitment are more likely to be based on management actions), for example, Dedobbeleer and Beland (1991) found that management concerns (perceptions of manage-ment attitudes towards safety practices, workers' safety and work leaders' behaviour) and management safety activities (exposure to instructions on the safety policy, availability of proper equipment) were best represented as a single factor 'management commitment'.

There is support within the literature on organisational culture: Schein (1992) suggests that the way in which senior managers instruct, reward, allocate their attention and behave under pressure, will be particularly salient in shaping organisational culture; Schneider and Rentsch (1988) indicate that the explicit ways that managers communicate what is important (stating goals, rewarding job behaviours, establishing policies and procedures, etc.) will contribute to the work climate.

Perceptions of the safety management system

The workers' experience of how the company's safety management system operates (including safety training; safety rules and procedures; provision and maintenance of safety equipment; accident-reporting; and safety representatives and committees) will influence their perceptions of its adequacy. Mearns *et al.* (2003) describe safety management practices as an 'indicator of the safety culture of upper management'.

Much of the input to the safety management system (SMS) is at senior management level, where major decisions about the policy, planning, resourcing and organisation of the SMS take place. From a functionalist perspective, the source of safety strategy is also the source of the safety culture, as the culture represents the strategy in action, yet the workforce has very little contact with this level of the SMS. Workforce experience of the SMS will be at the level of implementation (procedures, rules, regulations and standards for safe systems of work; maintenance; emergency exercises; training) and monitoring (audits/inspections; accident/incident/near-miss reporting); access to higher level input will depend on the safety information system, e.g. safety policy manual, feedback on reports and action records. Formal mechanisms may exist for the participation of the workforce in safety issues through safety representatives and safety committees.

Zohar (1980) found eight dimensions of safety climate, but only four of these were required to discriminate between factories: perceived importance of safety training programs; perceived effects of required workpace on safety; perceived status of safety officer; perceived status of safety committee. Three of these dimensions are related to perceptions of safety management. Cox *et al.* (1998)

found that quality of safety training was related to management actions for safety and both variables were significant predictors of appraisal of commitment. Cheyne *et al.* (1998) identify a major dimension of safety climate as 'safety management' which is characterised by items such as 'safety training has a high priority', 'there is a process of continual improvement' and 'line supervisors actively support safety'; this factor had an indirect impact on safety activities mediated by personal involvement and individual responsibility and several other pathways of influence, mediated by communication, workplace hazards and the physical work environment.

Lee (1998) describes several factors which focus on aspects of the SMS: confidence in safety procedures (related to management response to safety representatives and safety committees, reporting of near-misses, work done by safety representatives and committees, alarm systems, emergency procedures and identification of potential hazards); personal understanding of safety rules (instructions are not too detailed or too complicated); satisfaction with training (both general training and safety training). Each of these differentiates between high- and low-accident groups. Williamson *et al.* (1997) also identify a 'positive safety practice' factor, which includes items referring to safety equipment, safety training and safety rules and procedures. This factor differentiated between accident-involved and accident-free employees. Coyle *et al.*'s (1995) measure of safety climate contains several facets of the SMS: maintenance and management issues (e.g. 'how satisfactory is maintenance on equipment?'); company policy (e.g. 'how likely is it that you would be reprimanded for not using safety equipment or protective clothing?'); training (e.g. 'how would you rate the induction training you received?'); policy/procedures (e.g. 'how aware are you of emergency procedures in the event of fire/explosion?').

Safety attitudes of the workforce

Workers' safety attitudes and perceptions of risk at the workplace will be influenced by their personal beliefs about risk and safety; personal involvement; individual responsibility; evaluation of safety measures; and evaluation of the physical hazards of the workplace. Mearns *et al.* (2003) describe the safety climate as an 'indicator of safety culture within the workforce as a whole'.

Cox and Cox (1991) investigated the architecture of safety attitudes towards safety software, people and risk (excluding safety hardware or specific hazards); they found five dimensions: personal scepticism; individual responsibility; safeness of work environment; effectiveness of arrangements for safety; personal immunity. Cox and Cox describe individual responsibility (constructive belief), personal scepticism and immunity (both unconstructive beliefs) as personal beliefs about risk and safety, while safeness of the work environment and effectiveness of arrangements for safety are both evaluations. Cheyne *et al.* (1998) measured the physical work environment (basic environmental work conditions: lighting, ventilation, working space, humidity), physical hazards and attitudes to safety. Factor analysis of attitudes to safety found five dimensions: safety management; communication; individual responsibility; safety standards and goals; personal involvement. The model supported by Cheyne *et al.* (1998) indicates that individual responsibility mediates the relationship between personal involvement and safety activities; physical work environment has a direct effect on safety activities, while the relationship with workplace hazards is also mediated by individual responsibility. Fleming *et al.* (1998) looked at factors affecting risk perceptions: job situation (e.g. level of communication and work demands); safety satisfaction (confidence in post-accident and safety measures); job satisfaction; working environment (perceptions of the harshness of the environment); management commitment to safety; safety attitudes. Perceived risk of hazards to the individual was predicted by job situation, working environment, safety satisfaction and job satisfaction; work task hazards by all factors except job situation; and hazards to the platform by only working environment.

An overview of this research suggests that important attitudes and beliefs held by workers might be considered under the following headings:

- *Personal beliefs about risk and safety*: immunity/optimism (e.g. 'accidents only happen to other people'); scepticism/fatalism (e.g. 'if I worried about safety I would not get my job done') (Cox and Cox 1991; Williamson *et al.* 1997). These beliefs may be related to the personality variable 'safety locus of control' described by Jones and Wuebker (1985).
- *Personal actions/involvement*: degree of personal involvement (e.g. attendance of safety meetings) and personal actions (e.g. helping each other, reporting accidents/incidents). One would expect that the personality variable conscientiousness

would influence personal involvement (Robertson and Clarke 1999).

- *Individual responsibility*: a constructive belief (Cox and Cox 1991) including items such as 'safety equipment should always be worn' and also more action-oriented items, such as 'I can influence performance' (Cheyne *et al.* 1998). This is similar to a construct described by Coyle *et al.* (1995) as 'personal authority', which includes items such as, 'How confident are you in your ability to train someone else to do your job?' and 'To what extent are your opinions sought on potentially dangerous operating procedures?' As noted by Turner (1994) a degree of authority is needed to activate the motivation to care about safety.
- *Satisfaction with safety measures*: procedures, rules and regulations, safety measures, evacuation drills, etc.
- *Work environment/conditions*: physical work environment (e.g. lighting, ventilation) and job conditions (e.g. work demands).

'Perceptions of risk' feature strongly as a major dimension of safety climate (Zohar 1980; Brown and Holmes 1986; Dedobbeleer and Beland 1991; Diaz and Cabrera 1997). There is also empirical evidence to support a relationship between risk perceptions and accidents (Fleming *et al.* 1998), and between appraisals of the physical environment and safe behaviour (Tomas and Oliver 1995).

A number of studies have attempted to investigate the mechanisms by which elements of safety climate/safety culture affect safety outcomes, using statistical modelling techniques, such as structural equation modelling (SEM) and path analysis (Melia *et al.* 1992; Oliver *et al.* 1993; Witt *et al.* 1994; Tomas and Oliver 1995; Janssens *et al.* 1995; Flin *et al.* 1996; Thompson *et al.* 1998; Fleming *et al.* 1998; Cox *et al.* 1998; Cheyne *et al.* 1998; Oliver *et al.* 2002). These models show the relationships between the elements of safety climate; there is some degree of consensus that organisational factors influence individual safety attitudes, which in turn influence individual safety behaviour.

Research has tended to highlight workers' perceptions of the work environment (the safety climate) as the important influences on occupational safety. However, key relationships, between workers and managers, and also between workers and supervisors (though the latter has received less attention), will also affect safety performance, possibly mediated by the safety climate.

Leadership

Leadership style may have a particularly important effect on occupational safety, due to the influence of managers on the prevailing safety climate. For example, Denison (1996) states that climate is 'often subject to direct manipulation by people with power and influence'. Zohar (2002a) indicates that concern for the welfare of workers, which varies with transformational or trans-actional leadership styles (Bass 1990), provides a source for climate perceptions. Aspects of transformational leadership have been associated with lower accident rates (Barling *et al.* 2000, 2002; Yule 2002; Zohar 2002a). Transformational leadership has been defined in terms of four separate dimensions: *individualised consideration* (leader shows interest in the personal and professional development of subordinates); *intellectual stimulation* (leader challenges assumptions and encourages subordinates to be creative and innovative); *inspirational motivation* (leader inspires others towards goals and provides meaning, optimism and enthusiasm); and *idealised influence* (leader inspires confidence and is perceived as charismatic). There is empirical evidence to suggest that each of these dimensions has an effect on occupational safety.

Barling *et al.* (2000) used modified scales of transformational and constructive leadership (referring specifically to safety) for a sample of restaurant workers. They found that inspirational motivation and intellectual stimulation have an effect on safety performance because leaders challenge group members to go beyond individual needs for the collective good (resulting in organisational citizenship behaviours and safety participation). Idealised influence also has a significant effect by enhancing subordinates' perceptions of safety as a social responsibility. Yule (2002) found that two elements of transformational leadership style significantly correlated with lower accident rates (intellectual stimulation, $r = 0.508$, $p<0.01$, and individualised consideration, $r = 0.366$, $p<0.05$). Moreover, larger differences between the leaders' self-perception and their upward appraisal scores were significantly associated with higher accident rates. This suggests that managers who are less in touch with how their style is received generally lead businesses with poorer safety records. Zohar (2002a) argues that individualised consideration influences open, informal safety communication, which in turns affects injury rate. Greater concern for subordinates' welfare is based on closer individualised relationships, which promotes supervisory practices and, in turn affects safety behaviour.

Transactional leadership is associated with higher accident rates (Yule 2002). Corrective supervisors adjust performance standards according to their assigned priorities in which safety has no special status (Zohar 2002a). There is some 'compensation effect' from transformational leaders where safety priorities are low, as this results in managers becoming more concerned for their subordinates' welfare. Zohar (2003) suggests that in subunits where activity is more routinised work procedures are more formalised and 'routine but reliable' performance is necessary, safety compliance is more important than safety participation, and transactional supervision is needed; in fact, transformational may have negative effects due to emphasis on 'performance beyond expectations'.

O'Dea and Flin (2000) examined leadership style in a sample of offshore installation managers (OIMs) in charge of offshore oil and gas platforms. Although OIMs recognised that participative management activities, such as participation of workforce, open relationships, empowering employees, communication and listening to employees, were best practice for safety leadership, 57 per cent preferred a more authoritarian approach.

The literature suggests that leadership style may have differential effects dependent upon the distance between the leader and the subordinate (Shamir 1995). Griffin *et al.* (2002) found that their results indicated that senior and local leadership were positively and independently related to safety climate. Safety climate fully mediated the relationship between local leadership and safety behaviour, while senior leadership was only partially mediated by safety climate. Local leadership also moderated the link between safety climate and safety participation. Zohar (2002a) suggests that the practices of middle-level managers influence those of their immediate subordinates, influencing, in turn, their own subordinates (i.e. foremen and forewomen). The important role played by supervisors in occupational safety is often under-researched, in comparison to the influence of more senior managers.

Supervision

Supervisors act as role models for instilling safety awareness and supporting safe behaviour. Supervisors represent a source of workers' perceptions of management commitment, which receives little research attention. Thompson *et al.* (1998) examined supervisor support for safety separately from management support; they found that these two variables mediated different relationships: supervisor support mediated the relationship between supervisor fairness and safety compliance, while management support mediated the relationship between organisational politics and safety conditions. Safety attitude surveys are frequently confined to measuring the attitudes of workers; when supervisors' or managers' attitudes are included, participants are often few in number and merged into an overall analysis, rather than analysed separately. Studies report on hierarchical differences within the same factor structure (e.g. Hofmann and Stetzer 1996; Cox *et al.* 1998; Mearns *et al.* 1998) rather than examining separate factor structures; in an exception, Niskanen (1994) found that the factor structures for supervisors' attitudes and workers' attitudes were very similar. Supervisors may communicate management support for safety more directly than many management actions, e.g. reporting discipline/ compliance back to managers (Leather 1987; Kozlowski and Doherty 1989; Niskanen 1994; Thompson *et al.* 1998; Clarke 1999).

Recent safety research has focused on the quality of the relationship between local leaders and their subordinates (leader–member exchange). Leader–member exchange (LMX) theory is based on the idea that leaders differentiate between subordinates and this is reflected in the way that they supervise them. A high LMX relationship is characterised by mutual trust, loyalty and extra-role behaviours; a low LMX relationship is one that is within the bounds of the employment contract such that the employee performs his or her job, but contributes nothing extra. In a review, Schriesheim *et al.* (1999) argue that six dimensions are predominant in LMX research: *mutual support, trust, liking, latitude, attention* and *loyalty*. High LMX relationships have been associated with safety citizenship behaviour and higher safety commitment in subordinates (Hofmann *et al.* 2001).

Where trust for the leader is high, Mayer *et al.* (1995) found that leaders engaged in more 'risk-taking behaviours' (such as delegation and empowerment) and subordinates demonstrated organisational citizenship behaviours and enhanced performance. Further work by Davis *et al.* (2000) found a significant positive relationship between the level of trust in the general manager and restaurant performance. General managers who were perceived as trustworthy were also perceived as higher in ability, benevolence and integrity. The lack of high-quality exchange relationships is associated with negative consequences (not just the absence of positive effects).

Townsend *et al.* (2000) showed that performance and citizenship were positively related to LMX, but moreover, that LMX was *negatively* correlated with retaliation behaviour. In terms of safety, Hofmann and Morgeson (1999) found that employees who perceive the organisation as supportive and have high leader–member exchange more likely to raise safety concerns with their supervisor. Safety communication was related to safety commitment (as rated by the supervisor) and to accidents. However, although supervisors' response to safety is dependent on leadership style (concern for welfare of subordinates), it is also dependent upon externally assigned safety priorities (perceptions of superiors concern for safety). Therefore, as stated by O'Dea and Flin (2000: 53), supervisors are crucial, 'but their effectiveness hinges on the adequacy of their senior managers'.

Safety subclimates

Researchers have suggested that departments and work teams have distinct subunit climates (Joyce and Slocum 1984; Jackofsky and Slocum 1988). The existence of safety subcultures has been demonstrated in empirical studies (Guest *et al.* 1994; M. D. Cooper and Phillips 1994; Clarke 1998a). For example, Guest *et al.* (1994) compared the characteristics of high- and low-accident work groups (gangs of railway track workers) and found that 'safe' gangs were more cohesive, more considerate, more trusting of each other, more involved and interested in the work, and more reliable in following procedures. The differences were partly due to the different attitudes and actions of the supervisors of 'safe' gangs who were more concerned with their workers, made staff feel valued, kept them informed and treated them fairly. Thus, the leadership style of local management can have a significant impact on the safety performance of work groups. Hofmann and Stetzer (1996) examined group processes, as well as safety climate, in teams working in chemical processing plants. They found that group processes were related not only to group effectiveness, but also to safety-related outcomes of the group. Despite the previous research that suggests the importance of safety subclimates, researchers have tended to focus on measuring safety climate at an individual level, but aggregating individual responses to determine safety climate at an organisational level. Guldenmund (2000) notes that respondents are more likely to use their own personal experience, rather than abstract references to the whole organisation, to answer questions, even where explicitly requested to do otherwise.

Zohar (2000) conducted a multilevel investigation of the sources of workers' safety perceptions; in this study, supervisory actions and attitudes are identified as a source of climate perceptions at the *group level*. Supervisors execute management policies and procedures on the shop floor and 'workers interpret supervisory action in individual role episodes as reflecting an overall emphasis or de-emphasis on safety issues' (Zohar 2000: 588). Given that prescriptive rules and regulations cannot cover every eventuality, supervisory discretion will influence the prioritisation of safety in employees' work. This was supported by the finding of high within-group homogeneity and significant between-groups variation in terms of the level of 'microaccidents' (minor injuries) experienced by work groups (Zohar 2000). The results confirm that perceptions of patterns of supervisory action (i.e. group level safety climate) have an impact on worker behaviour and accident rates. In a later study, Zohar (2002b), line supervisors received weekly feedback based on episodic interviews with subordinates concerning the cumulative frequency of their safety oriented interactions. An intervention was introduced to increase the number of safety oriented interactions supervisors initiated. A significant increase in this type of supervisory practice was accompanied by significant (and stable) changes in minor injury rate, earplug use and safety climate scores.

Summary

Much of the literature related to accident causation has emphasised the role of environmental and organisational level factors, particularly the safety culture and climate. Workers' perceptions of management commitment, the safety management system and individual responsibility for safety emerge as important variables. More recently, researchers have linked safety climate with general organisational climate and structure, including leadership and supervision. The individual contribution to accidents has been neglected in much of the safety literature. The relationship between accident involvement and psychological factors is discussed in Chapter 4.

Psychological factors and occupational safety

The growing emphasis on the importance of organisational and management factors in occupational safety, discussed in the previous chapter, has led to the relative neglect of psychological factors related to the individual. This chapter presents an overview of these variables, including human factors and individual differences, and how they are related to safety at both an individual and an organisational level.

Human factors

Much of the earliest research examining the causation of accidents focused on *human factors*, with a particular emphasis on identifying defects of cognition, attention, perception or intelligence related to accidents. Researchers discovered that there is unequal liability to accident involvement (Newbold 1927; Farmer and Chambers 1926) and concluded that this variation is related to individual differences. Significant differences in intelligence, skills and personality have been found between accident and non-accident groups of pilots, for example, supporting the human factors explanation (Biesheuvel and White 1949).

Human factors have been identified as relating to driving ability and road traffic accidents (e.g. Porter 1988; Arthur *et al.* 1991; Evans 1991; McKenna *et al.* 1986). Brown (1990) suggests that attentional errors account for 40 per cent of road accidents, perceptual errors for a further 25 per cent and judgemental errors account for another 10–15 per cent of accidents.

There is limited evidence for a relationship with *information-processing* or *cognitive ability* and accidents. Arthur *et al.* (1991) conducted a meta-analytic review of information-processing and cognitive ability variables: selective attention, perceptual style, choice and complex reaction time. The study found small effect sizes for choice and complex reaction time (0.05) and also for perceptual style (0.15). Although some studies have supported a relationship with information-processing, e.g. Avolio *et al.* (1985) found significant correlations between six measures of information processing and accidents (from 0.13 to 0.43), other studies have found little or no relationship (e.g. McKenna *et al.* 1986). McKenna *et al.* (1986) found that there was no significant relationship between either cognitive abilities or intelligence with the accident involvement of bus drivers over a two-year period.

The evidence for the role of *attention* in driving accidents is inconclusive. Evans (1991) suggests that there is no systematic relationship between visual performance and driving ability; however, Porter (1988) reported that poor visual attention and experience of major life events were most consistently related to accidents. Arthur *et al.* (1994) also support a relationship between visual attention and driving accidents. They found significant correlations between three versions of a computer-based visual attention test (from 0.26 to 0.38) between errors on visual attention scores and self-reported driving accidents. Although Arthur *et al.* (1991) found little evidence of a relationship between cognitive ability or perceptual style and driving accidents, the evidence for auditory selective attention was more convincing (0.26).

Human error

Reason (1990) identifies three basic human error types: slips, lapses and mistakes. Slips and lapses are execution failures, where actions fail to occur as intended. *Slips* result from attentional failures, whereas *lapses* are failures of storage (memory failures). *Mistakes* are planning failures, where intended actions fail to achieve their desired outcomes.

Wagenaar and Groeneweg (1987) investigated maritime accidents and identified five general types of human error: wrong habits, wrong diagnoses, lack of attention, lack of training and unsuitable personality. However, they found that the accidents they investigated were often the result of several people's errors, rather than the errors of one individual. The way in which these errors combined could not have been anticipated and, indeed, before the occurrence of the accident, would have been deemed impossible. They conclude that accidents 'do not occur because people gamble and lose, they occur because people do not believe that the accident about to occur is at all possible' (Wagenaar and Groeneweg 1987: 596). The accidents had the following factors in common:

- highly complex coincidences are rarely foreseeable by those involved;
- unpredictability due to the large number of causes and spread of information over the participants;
- lack of understanding rather than motivation or risk propensity;
- the behaviours were not previously seen as risky.

An analysis of the human errors that contributed to the accidents showed that *cognitive factors* accounted for 70 per cent of errors and were involved in 93 per cent of accidents (false hypotheses 51 per cent; habits 46 per cent; information-processing, especially attention 35 per cent; training 35 per cent; personality 35 per cent). *Social factors* contributed to 21 per cent of accidents (mostly due to social pressure), with *situational factors* contributing to 56 per cent (ergonomics being the most prominent factor, 34 per cent). The scenario that occurred most frequently was when an information-processing error was coupled with situational stress, particularly when lack of attention was combined with poor visibility.

These results were largely replicated in further studies reported by Groeneweg (1992). Accidents in the Dutch police force and an oil company produced similar results, with 71 per cent cognitive errors (in 96 per cent of all accidents) in the police study (the main factors being information-processing and false hypotheses, although the social system, in the form of social role, also scored highly) and 55 per cent cognitive errors (in 100 per cent of all accidents) in the oil company study (mainly, false hypotheses and habit, with an approximately equal role played by ergonomics and environmental stress).

Studies in other occupational areas have also highlighted the role of cognitive factors, particularly false hypotheses and inattention. For example, several studies have examined the reasons that train drivers pass signals at danger (e.g. Davis 1958; Buck 1963; Davis 1966; van der Flier and Schoonman 1988; Gilchrist *et al.* 1989). The study conducted by van der Flier and Schoonman (1988) examined the circumstances of 224 signals passed at danger (SPADs) over a two-year period (1983–4) on Dutch Railways. The causes associated with driver error included the following (percentage of incidents classified under cause in brackets; incidents could be classified under more than one cause):

- stop signal not noticed   (31.7 per cent)
- stop signal noticed too late   (25.5 per cent)
- previous signal not noticed   (6.7 per cent)
- incorrect anticipation of signal   (10.7 per cent)
- having been distracted   (11.2 per cent)
- faulty braking   (10.7 per cent)

The first five causes are all perceptual errors that are related to the mechanisms of false hypotheses and preoccupation. 'False hypotheses' can take a number of forms, but generally occur when people respond to situations as they conceive them, not as they really are (Davis 1958). The hypothesis 'governs the way in which [a person] perceives the situation and the way in which he organises the perceptual material available to him' (Davis 1958: 25). The persistence of a false hypothesis can be strengthened under a number of conditions, two of which are particularly relevant on the railway. First, is the condition of strong expectation and can be based on past experience or an appraisal of the current situation. This has a particularly strong effect, and has been shown to persist even when the signal is strong and of some duration. Second, is the effect of 'specific end deterioration' which occurs when anxiety is low, particularly after a period of stress.

A further study was carried out on British Rail (Gilchrist *et al.* 1989). The primary finding of this investigation was that the major causation of 88 per cent of SPAD cases examined (eighty-eight cases in the period 1986–9) was driver error. Physical influences (which were found to account for the remaining 12 per cent of SPADs) were grouped into effects of the environment and equipment. The categorisation of the causative factors in SPADs was as follows:

- *knowledge*: gaps in knowledge about route, traction, procedures
- *anticipation*: that a signal will clear
- *assumption*: that a signal is clear
- *miscommunication*: verbal, hand signal, telephone misunderstandings
- *inattention*: distraction by worries, cab-riders, lineside, etc.

- *low arousal*: due to fatigue, drugs, alcohol, etc.
- *equipment*: substandard equipment
- *environment*: severe weather conditions.

Knowledge, anticipation and assumption all relate to false hypotheses; inattention and low arousal belong to the category of preoccupation; in addition, miscommunication is identified as a factor. Further evidence for the role of inattention and preoccupation is provided by Haga (1984) who found that signal vigilance errors in train drivers were related to failures of sustained attention, particularly influenced by distraction. Smiley (1990) concluded that the failure of sustained attention was a major contributing factor in the Hinton train disaster (however, the cab environment was not conducive to good vigilance performance).

The human factors identified as underlying driver errors on the railways correspond to those found by Wagenaar and Groeneweg (1987). The five human factors that contributed to maritime accidents were deficiencies in habits, defective diagnoses, lack of attention, inadequate training and unsuitable personality. On the railways, errors were related to false hypotheses and inattention. Similar factors have been indicated by Langham *et al.* (2002), looking at the causes of collisions with highly conspicuous police vehicles parked on the hard shoulder of a motorway. These collisions were the result of vigilance failure and false hypotheses about road conditions (e.g. drivers would assume the vehicle was moving, not stationary) rather than sensory failure.

One conclusion that can be drawn from reviewing the previous evidence is that errors due to inattention and false hypotheses tend to occur when the individual is behaving at a routine level. Experience of a situation that is generally predictable and repetitive will result in tasks being performed at the *skill-based level* (Rasmussen 1982), that is, actions that were once consciously monitored and carried out one at a time will become automatically performed sequences of action. Edkins and Pollock (1997) found that train driver errors occurred most frequently at the skill-based level (59 per cent) and that inattention was the most common psychological factor (70 per cent). Hobbs and Williamson (2002) also found a high number of skill-based errors in aircraft maintenance. They concluded that this occurs due to the greater opportunity for skill-based errors in routine work, rather than the skill-based level being intrinsically unreliable. Although skill-based performance is generally reliable, it gives rise to certain predictable types of error (Reason 1990).

The development of skill has several effects: individual actions within a well-practised block of actions will be started before the environment requires them, i.e. there is anticipation; once started, blocks of action are not monitored for their effects on the environment; the performance of practised action gives the impression of having plenty of time as it requires little conscious effort; performance is dissociated from intention as actions will respond to situational cues rather than conscious intent (Broadbent 1987). The knowledge used in skill-based action is implicit to the person–environment interaction that forms the unit of its performance. Thus, the person's implicit knowledge of what to do is prompted by the situation and has meaning only in relation to that particular interaction with the environment. Skill-based behaviour is basically a sequence of set actions interspersed with attentional checks. Behaviour proceeds in preprogrammed sequences until a point is reached where there is a choice of actions. It is at these points where conscious attention is given to what the person is doing to check that he or she is about to embark on the correct sequence. Errors occur when these attentional checks are misplaced (overattention), e.g. a skilled pianist checks the positioning of her fingers during an arpeggio and disrupts her playing, and when they are omitted at proper check points (inattention). The latter kind of error is the more common (Reason 1990).

A moment of inattention can result in a number of errors (*slips* of action and *lapses* of memory): double-capture slips, omissions following interruptions, reduced intentionality, perceptual confusions and interference errors (see Norman 1981; Reason 1990 for further details). Reduced intentionality occurs when there is a delay between deciding to do something and actually doing it. Perceptual confusions involve accepting things as correct when they are only similar to what is intended. Interference errors involve the mixing up of two action sequences or actions in a single sequence (the verbal example of this is a 'spoonerism'). Double-capture slips are most common and frequently take the form of *strong-but-wrong* actions. The circumstances for such errors are described by Reason (1990: 42) as follows: 'all that is required to elicit a "strong-but-wrong" action sequence is the omission (or misapplication) of an attentional check in circumstances where some departure from previous routine was intended or necessary'. Strong habit intrusions occur where an often performed action sequence takes over instead of the intended, but less frequent, one.

It is important that psychological factors are not viewed as operating independently from the organisational context. Edkins and Pollock (1997) noted that staff attitudes were related to 31 per cent of all latent failures (including low morale, complacency and overfamiliarity with the job, lack of pride, poor motivation, taking short cuts). Van der Flier and Schoonman (1988) found that previous accidents and lower job satisfaction were significantly predictive of future SPAD incidents and Kogi (1972) supported a relationship between staff indifference (attitude to their job) and greater vigilance decrement.

Violations

In a study looking at the unsafe acts committed by motorists, Reason *et al.* (1990) found evidence for three distinct categories of aberrant behaviour: violations, dangerous errors and relatively harmless lapses. *Violations* are deviations from safe operating procedures; while such actions are deliberate, they do not usually have a malevolent intent (this would be sabotage). Lapses were the most frequently reported driver errors (reported most by women), while violations and dangerous errors were less frequent (with more violations being reported by men). Young men were the group who reported violating the most. It was suggested that because violations were found to decrease with age, but errors remained stable, the two categories have different underlying causes. In addition, it was found that drivers with a high violation score, rather than a high error score, were involved in the most accidents.

Reason *et al.* (1990) have suggested that the psychological processes underlying the commission of errors and violations are fundamentally different. Errors are said to result from faulty information-processing at an individual level, whereas violations 'can only be described with regard to a social context in which behaviour is governed by operating procedures, codes of practice, rules, norms and the like' (Reason *et al.* 1990: 1,316). The infringement of safety rules are not usually acts of deliberate risk taking, but short cuts designed to make work more efficient, quicker, or easier (Reason *et al.* 1994). As operators are not able to assess the impact of violations on the system as a whole, their actions are often reinforced as there are no obvious or immediate negative consequences. Reason *et al.* (1994) identify three types of violations: routine (short cuts that become a habitual part of behavioural repertoire); optimising (serve non-functional goals, such as joy of speed or aggression, become part of individual's performance style); situational (non-compliance needed to get the job done).

The commission of violations in the workplace may result in either correct or incorrect performance (Reason *et al.* 1998). Correct performance is associated with accurate hazard perception, task training, learning from experience and organisational factors (such as leadership, supervisory example, etc). Reason *et al.* (1998) argue that correct actions are based on the individual conducting an accurate hazard evaluation of prevailing local conditions, and acting in accordance with the level of risk. The inclusion of risk perception blurs the distinction between errors and violations (Reason *et al.* 1990) by recognising that some actions may involve a deviation from procedures (violation), but are based on inaccurate judgements about the consequences (mistake) resulting in *misventions*. Correct violations, such as breaking a rule because an assessment of localised hazards indicates the rule is inappropriate, will demand that individuals are given the latitude to make decisions; they must be appropriately trained and empowered in order to accurately assess and evaluate hazards.

A further dimension affecting the commission of violations is *psychological rewards*. Individuals are more likely to violate safety rules where psychological rewards, fulfilling personal goals, are attached. Correct compliance is undermined where the behaviour required is correct but psychologically unrewarding. Such behaviours are likely to become extinct, as the temptation to violate the rule is too much (e.g. wearing uncomfortable personal protective equipment, such as gloves or masks). Reason *et al.* (1998: 296) note that such violations may seem innocuous, but can have negative effects: 'incorrect but psychologically rewarding violations are the breed stock from which occasional misventions emerge. Though often inconsequential in themselves, they create the conditions that promote dangerous misventions, particularly overconfidence in personal skills and an underestimation of the hazards'.

Although they have been considered as independent unsafe acts, accidents often result from a combination of errors and violations. Brown (1990) suggests that motorists have a bias towards 'inadequate safety margins'. Driving with an insufficient margin for safety means that certain types of error become more likely. Motorists who violate the accepted rules of the road, by speeding or following too close, reduce their safety margin, and in so doing, create a self-imposed time constraint. Thus, drivers have less time to assess the situation (leading to attentional errors); less time to process incoming information (leading to perceptual errors); and a limited opportunity to appreciate the potential danger of a situation (leading to judgemental errors). Thus, drivers who violate create a situation for themselves where their likelihood of making an error is much increased. Fergenson (1971) found a significant interaction between accidents and violations, such that high violators with lower cognitive efficiency had a high accident rate whereas as those with a zero accident rate were significantly better at processing information. This would suggest that while violations reduce the safety margin for all drivers, it is those who are least able to deal with the increased cognitive load who are most susceptible to errors. Reason *et al.* (1990) found that error proneness was a significant predictor of dangerous errors and less dangerous lapses. Although mood was also a significant predictor of errors (and violations), error proneness, which is characterised by higher rates of absent-mindedness and inattention, can be treated as a relatively enduring individual characteristic as it is stable over time (Broadbent *et al.* 1982).

Accident proneness

One causative explanation for the involvement of individuals in multiple accidents is the existence of an *accident proneness* trait, a concept introduced by Greenwood and Woods (1919). The finding that certain employees were consistently involved in a high number of accidents (e.g. Newbold 1926) supported the proposal that certain individuals were more likely to be involved in accidents due to a permanent trait (Farmer and Chambers 1926). Researchers have linked various personality traits with accident repeaters (LeShan 1952; Davids and Mahoney 1957; Kunce 1967). High accident rates were found to be associated with low trust, low optimism, resentment and negative employment attitudes (LeShan 1952) and also with high impulsiveness and risk-taking (Kunce 1967). Miner and Brewer (1983: 1,004) describe accident proneness as a transient personality maladjustment that particularly affects young people rather than a permanent trait, where 'the major motivation behind the repeated accidents themselves appears to be a desire to impress others by resorting to sudden and very risky decisions and behaviour'. However, rigorous statistical testing of the accident proneness hypothesis shed doubt on its validity (e.g. Smeed 1960); Hale and Hale (1972) have argued that it is an artefact of inadequate control of confounding factors such as age, tenure, occupation and exposure to risk.

Further research revived interest in individual differences as causative factors in accidents (e.g. McKenna 1983). Research by Boyle (1980) using the 'found experiment' technique, showed that individuals were differentiated with respect to their accident rates, with controls for ambient risk levels, exposure to risk, age and job experience. Boyle found that there was a significant correlation between accidents in the first and second halves of the eight-year period over which records had been kept. A study by Porter and Corlett (1989) found two distinct groups of individuals based on responses to their accident proneness questionnaire. These two groups were distinguished by their beliefs about their own accident proneness. One group (APS) believed they were prone to everyday minor accidents (such as tripping, cutting or bruising oneself, or breaking an object); the second group (NAPS) believed they were not prone to such accidents. It was found that the APS subjects performed significantly worse on the primary task (a computer-based unidimensional tracking task) of a dual task experiment. Such results indicate that there may be performance differences based on individual characteristics.

There are many problems with the concept of accident proneness, for example, whether it is a single personality trait or a number of different personality traits (Shaw and Sichel 1971) or, whether it is stable across situations or over time (Adelstein 1952; Guilford 1973; Shaw and Sichel 1971). In light of these difficulties, some researchers have concluded that it is not possible to isolate accident prone individuals: 'psychologists are talking moonshine if they claim that accident-prone people can be removed through psychological testing' (Wagenaar and Groeneweg 1987). Accident proneness may be a transient state, experienced by many people at some point in their lives, rather than a permanent trait, likened by Reason (1990) to a club with an ever-changing membership.

Personality characteristics

Despite the lack of faith in the concept of accident proneness, there is a body of empirical work that links some personality traits with accident involvement. An early literature review by Keehn (1961) concluded that extraversion, possibly accompanied by neurosis, is associated with higher accident liability. A more recent review by Hansen (1988) identified six personality categories where there is empirical support for an association with greater accident involvement: external locus of control, extraversion, aggression, social maladjustment, neuroticism and impulsivity. Many studies that examine the relationship between personality and accident involvement have focused upon road traffic accidents. A meta-analysis conducted by Arthur et al. (1991) reviewed this literature and found small–moderate effect sizes for four personality categories: locus of control (0.20); regard for authority (0.16); general activity level (0.07); level of distress (0.02).

One of the difficulties with personality studies is that they have lacked a coherent taxonomy, resulting in a wide variety of personality traits being measured, using a mixture of different types of methodology. Older studies, until the 1970s, used questionnaires (e.g. Katz adjustment scales), projective tests (e.g. TAT, Rorschach) and clinical interviews, while more recent studies favour personality inventories, such as 16PF. The personality traits measured include extraversion, neuroticism, social maladjustment, aggression, impulsivity, locus of control, sensation-seeking and, more recently, positive affectivity/negative affectivity and Type A behaviour. In order to clarify the existing literature, Robertson and Clarke (2002) conducted a meta-analysis of personality and occupational accidents, using the 'big five' taxonomy to categorise personality traits. The results revealed criterion-related validity (uncorrected) for four of the big five factors: (low) agreeableness, openness, neuroticism and (low) conscientiousness (with uncorrected mean validities of 0.32, 0.29, 0.19 and 0.15 respectively). These indicated that individuals high in openness and neuroticism, and low in agreeableness and conscientiousness, are more liable to be accident involved. The validities are similar in magnitude to previous meta-analyses in relation to vehicular accident involvement (Arthur et al. 1991) and job performance (Barrick and Mount 1991). Following the lead of Robertson and Clarke (2002), the following sections review the evidence relating personality to accidents, by looking at each of the 'big five' personality dimensions in turn.

Extraversion

Eysenck (1962) proposed that extraverts have a lower level of vigilance, and will be less involved in tasks, and therefore more liable to be involved in accidents. Several empirical studies have supported this assertion, for example, Powell *et al.* (1971) found that the number of accidents experienced by mill workers was significantly higher for extraverts. However, much of the support for extraversion as a predictor of accident involvement has derived from traffic accidents, where extraverts are significantly more accident involved (Fine 1963; Smith and Kirkham 1981; Arthur and Graziano 1996). A few studies have found the opposite effect, where introverts are more accident involved (Pestonjee and Singh 1980; Roy and Choudhary 1985). It is possible that this may be a cultural effect, as the latter studies all involved Indian participants, whereas empirical support for extraverts being more accident involved derives from studies with Western samples, including US, British and Australian.

Extraversion is a fairly broad personality category that includes a number of lower level facets: warmth, gregariousness, assertiveness, activity, excitement-seeking and positive emotions (Costa and McCrae 1985). Some authors have suggested that extraversion should be subdivided, for example, affiliation (sociable, gregarious, outgoing), achievement (ambitious, confident, hardworking) and potency (forceful, optimistic, vital) (Hough 1992). A number of lower level facets have been investigated with regard to accident liability. Loo (1979) found that impulsiveness was related to risky driving, whereas sociability was not (both facets of extraversion).

Iverson and Erwin (1997) found that positive affectivity (PA) had a significant negative correlation with accidents. They suggest that the more socially adjusted aspects of extraversion, as reflected in positive affectivity, will mitigate against accident involvement, as high positive affectivity is associated with greater self-efficacy (George and Brief 1992; Judge 1993), which is reflected in a higher degree of task engagement. They also suggest that high PA individuals will have more accurate and systematic decision-making skills (requesting information, recognising situational contingencies, and using data) (Staw and Barsade 1993), which is reflected in more thoughtful and careful appraisal of situations, reducing their accident risk.

Studies examining sensation-seeking, measured by Zuckerman Sensation-Seeking Scales (Zuckerman 1979), have generally supported a relationship with accident involvement (Jonah 1997). In a review of forty studies, Jonah (1997) found that the majority supported positive relationships between sensation seeking and risky driving, with correlations between 0.30 and 0.40. Iversen and Rundmo (2002) found that risk-taking behaviour was a major predictor of accident involvement, and this behaviour was associated with those who scored high on sensation-seeking, normlessness and driver anger. There is less empirical evidence to suggest a relationship with occupational accidents, although Lubner (1992) found that US pilots involved in aviation accidents scored significantly higher on thrill and adventure-seeking.

Although the role of extraversion in accident involvement is largely supported in the safety literature, the meta-analysis conducted by Robertson and Clarke (2002) indicated some contrary evidence. However, the importance of extraversion in occupational accidents may emerge at more senior levels, as Barrick and Mount (1991) have linked this personality characteristic with managerial performance.

Neuroticism

According to Eysenck (1970), neurotics will be more accident involved. Hansen (1989) suggests that neurotics are more distractible, being preoccupied with anxieties and worries, and therefore are involved in more accidents. There is also evidence that neurotics are less likely to seek active control of the environment (Judge 1993). A number of studies support a relationship between neuroticism, characterised by anxiety, hostility, depression, self-consciousness and impulsiveness, and accidents. Empirical support is found for professional drivers (Pestonjee and Singh 1980; Roy and Choudhary 1985), motorists (Selzer et al. 1968; Mayer and Treat 1977) and within industrial settings (Hansen 1989).

The tendency to experience negative emotions (negative affectivity) has a significant positive relationship with occupational injuries (Iverson and Erwin 1997). The authors suggest that not only are neurotics more distractible, but also they prefer less direct coping strategies, such as emotion-focused coping (Parkes 1990) increasing their accident risk. Neuroticism was the strongest single predictor of driver stress (Matthews *et al.* 1991), suggesting that neurotics may respond more negatively to the presence of stressors, increasing their vulnerability to accidents. This is supported by Sutherland and Cooper (1991), who examined neuroticism in offshore oil workers: high neurotics were involved in significantly more accidents, and were also more dissatisfied, reported lower mental health and were more likely to be heavy drinkers when onshore.

The meta-analysis conducted by Robertson and Clarke (2002) found some evidence of the relationship between neuroticism and occupational accidents. However, the influence of neuroticism may be disguised by the use of linear statistical methods. Lajunen (2001) found that neuroticism had a non-linear relationship with traffic accidents, such that both high and low neuroticism was associated with greater accident involvement. A further explanation is related to reporting bias, such that more neurotic individuals may have a greater tendency to report accidents; however, Robertson and Clarke (2002) note that this would be reflected in actual, rather than perceived, reports as all but two studies in the meta-analysis used archival rather than self-report accident data.

Conscientiousness

Meta-analyses (Barrick and Mount 1991; Tett *et al.* 1991) have reported a tendency for conscientiousness to correlate well across criterion measures of job performance. Barrick and Mount (1991) suggested that this personality dimension may act as a 'general' personality factor (akin to 'g' in cognitive ability). However, it may not be desirable in all occupational fields, such as managerial performance (Robertson *et al.* 2000). There is evidence to suggest a role for conscientiousness in terms of safety performance, with empirical studies supporting significant negative correlations between conscientiousness and accidents (Arthur and Graziano 1996; Cellar *et al.* 2001).

The definition of conscientiousness includes a number of different aspects: competence, order, dutifulness, achievement striving, self-discipline and deliberation. Goldberg (1990) describes the conscientious person as organised, conforming, detail conscious and dependable. There is evidence that several relevant personality traits, which relate to low scores on conscientiousness, are significantly associated with accident involvement. Low scores on 'self-discipline' relate to carelessness and a lack of self-control (Suchman 1970; Shaw and Sichel 1971) and low scores on 'cautiousness' to impulsivity (Mayer and Treat 1977). A further aspect of conscientiousness, related to deliberation and order, is reflected in thoroughness in decision-making style; low thoroughness has been shown to correlate with accident risk (West et al. 1993). Low thoroughness is characterised by a lack of forward planning, absence of a logical or systematic approach to decision making and inadequate cost–benefit analysis and contingency planning.

A low score on the facet of 'dutifulness' relates to a lack of respect for authority and social order: social maladjustment (Hansen 1989); social rebellion and antagonism to authority (Shaw and Sichel 1971); antisocial tendencies (Mayer and Treat 1977); social deviance (West et al. 1993). Evidence from West et al. (1993) suggests that social deviance increases traffic accident risk partly due to its association with increased driving speed. Two possible explanations are proposed: first, that exceeding speed limits involves breaking the law and individuals with higher social deviance have less regard for authority; second, social deviance may be caused by a stronger focus on immediate needs (such as making good progress) irrespective of possible future consequences for oneself or others (such as the adverse consequences of an accident). The latter explanation is reflected in 'optimising' violations (Reason et al. 1994), which serve non-functional goals, such as joy of speed or aggression, and become part of the individual's performance style. Those individuals who are higher in social deviance (low conscientiousness) would be more likely to engage in this type of rule-related behaviour. There is consistent evidence that violations are associated with increased accident risk in motorists (Parker et al. 1995) and truck drivers (Sullman et al. 2002), although little research has been conducted in workplace settings.

Individual differences may also affect the development of attitudes towards safety. Although few models include individual difference variables, Cheyne et al. (1998) suggest that 'individual responsibility' plays an important mediating role between organisational and environmental factors and individual behaviour. Given that more conscientious individuals are respectful of authority, they may also be predisposed towards the formation of such attitudes as 'individual responsibility'.

Reason *et al.* (1998: 300) suggest that 'mispliances are likely to be associated with the personal characteristics of rigid compliance ("rules must be obeyed at all times")'. This suggests that while high conscientiousness would normally be associated with less accident risk, extreme conscientiousness could have the opposite effect, as 'mispliances' involve obeying rules, even where the procedure was not appropriate for the situation (incorrect action). The extent to which high conscientiousness is desirable will also depend on the requirements of the job: more highly routinised and formalised work will require reliable performance and safety compliance, and therefore, high conscientiousness. This personality characteristic may have lower importance in less formalised work.

Agreeableness

People who are high on agreeableness are pleasant, tolerant, tactful, helpful, not defensive and generally easy to get along with (Hough 1992). There is some empirical evidence to support a negative relationship between agreeableness and accident involvement (Cellar *et al.* 2001), although other studies have found no association (Arthur and Graziano 1996).

Agreeableness includes elements of trust, compliance and altruism that are reflected in studies examining personality and accidents. Davids and Mahoney (1957) found a significant negative relationship between trust and accident involvement in workers at a US process engineering plant. Studies measuring low 'altruism', egocentricity (Davids and Mahoney 1957; Shaw 1965; Conger *et al.* 1959) and selfishness (Shaw and Sichel 1971), have all supported a significant positive relationship with accident involvement. The opposite pole of 'compliance' encompasses belligerence, hostility and aggression, all of which have been examined in relation to accident involvement. High aggression has been associated with greater accident involvement in railway workers (Sah 1989), US airmen (Conger *et al.* 1959) and Indian bus drivers (Roy and Choudary 1985). There is also evidence to suggest that high levels of aggression and hostility are associated with road accidents (Suchman 1970; Hemenway and Solnick 1993; Norris *et al.* 2000), although Vavrik (1997) found no significant relationship. A review of the literature concluded that hostile and aggressive tendencies are associated with greater accident liability (Beirness 1993). The link between driver anger and subsequent near accidents on the road

(Underwood *et al.* 1999) would suggest that drivers who become angered, and respond aggressively, are more likely to have accidents. However, studies have generally found that 'ordinary' violations (e.g. speeding) are significantly predictive of crash involvement (Meadows *et al.* 1998; Parker *et al.* 1995) rather than 'aggressive' violations (e.g. expressing hostility to another road user) (Sullman *et al.* 2002).

Robertson and Clarke (2002) found that low agreeableness was associated with accident involvement, a finding that is largely supported in traffic psychology, as aggressive individuals commit more violations and are more likely to be involved in road accidents. Yet, this does not appear to be just a 'road rage' effect, as Robertson and Clarke (2002) found a moderate effect for agreeableness in the context of occupational accidents. Agreeableness is most salient in situations that involve interaction or cooperation with others (Barrick and Mount 1991). Thus, reduced accident liability may reflect an enhanced ability to work with others effectively, e.g. altruistic tendencies allow the individual to consider the impact of their behaviour on others.

Openness

Openness is one of the least studied of the 'big five' personality dimensions in terms of job performance. Likewise, there are fewer studies that focus on openness and accident involvement, compared to the other personality dimensions. Arthur and Graziano (1996) found little evidence of a relationship between openness and self-reported traffic accidents; however, other studies have examined some of the facets of openness. High scorers on openness are imaginative, unconventional, curious, broadminded and cultured. Suhr (1961) found a negative relationship between imagination and accidents, but a positive relationship was found by Lardent (1991). Positive relationships have been supported between artistic, literary and aesthetic interests and accident involvement (Conger *et al.* 1957; Parker 1953). Meta-analyses (Barrick and Mount 1991; Salgado 1997) have supported a relationship between openness and training proficiency, indicating that high openness is associated with a positive disposition towards learning. Thus, high openness would be desirable for developing a well-trained workforce. However, particularly in a routinised working environment, where safety compliance is critical, more imaginative, curious and unconventional individuals may be more liable to rule violations, experimentation and improvisation. Low scorers on openness would have an enhanced ability to focus on the task in hand and, therefore, are less likely to become accident involved.

Evidence from road traffic studies suggests that violations, incidents and accidents on the roads are strongly related to risk taking behaviour (Jonah 1986; Iversen and Rundmo 2002). However, several authors, who have analysed the underlying causes of industrial accidents, have emphasised the lack of conscious risk taking in behaviour that leads to accidents (e.g. Reason 1990; Wagenaar 1992). This may suggest that different personality traits may be underlying safety-related behaviours in different contexts. Lajunen (2001) notes that, comparing data across thirty-four nations, while the personality traits of extraversion and neuroticism are related to road traffic accidents, they were unrelated to occupational fatalities. This may suggest that the personality traits associated with road traffic accidents differ from occupational accidents.

Risk propensity

There is a widely held view that accidents happen because individuals fail to accurately assess the danger inherent in a situation, or correctly perceive the danger and take a conscious risk. However, Wagenaar (1992) argues that much everyday behaviour is conducted without conscious evaluation of the risk involved, rather behaviour is automatic and shaped by past experience. Accidents are not caused by misperceptions of risk or conscious risk taking because behaviour is based on habit, particularly in routine situations. For example, in an analysis of fifty-seven accidents at sea, less than 1 per cent were caused by an individual consciously accepting a risky course of action (Wagenaar and Groeneweg 1987).

Fleming et al. (1998) found empirical evidence to support a relationship between risk perceptions (of hazards to the individual) and accidents. Higher risk perceptions (feeling less safe) were significantly related to job situation (felt less in control), working environment (felt more harsh), satisfaction with safety (felt less satisfied) and job satisfaction (felt less satisfied) (explained 22 per cent of variance). However, while risk perceptions were related to accidents, the contribution of risk perception, safety attitudes and safety satisfaction accounted for only 3 per cent of the variance.

Wagenaar (1992) suggests that while operators run risks, it is those placed higher in the organisational hierarchies that actually take risks. However, the literature concerning the risky decision-making of managers suggests *habitual behaviour* is also a significant factor. There is consistent evidence that inertia (habitual response to risk) and outcome history are both related to risk propensity (Pablo 1997; Sitkin and Weingart 1995). More experienced decision-makers may focus on their past ability to cope with obstacles, raising their level of confidence, and increasing the likelihood of risk behaviour and also less experienced individuals may have raised levels of confidence because of their lack of knowledge of the possible consequences of their actions (also leading to riskier behaviour). There is also evidence to suggest that organisational factors (industry, governmental control) have a direct effect on risk propensity (Williams and Narendran 1999). The organisational culture will influence managerial decision-making, dependent on the cultural value attached to risk seeking/uncertainty or risk avoidance/certainty. The risk climate within which the manager operates will provide a frame of reference for behaviour and indicate the acceptability of risk behaviour.

Decision-making within teams can be affected by an inadequate assessment and evaluation of risks. Janis (1972) examined the decision-making of small elite groups that resulted in planning deficiencies ultimately causing major catastrophes. Such defective decision-making was dubbed *groupthink* and defined as 'a deterioration of mental efficiency, reality testing and moral judgement that results from in-group pressures' (Janis 1972: 9). Groupthink is thought to stem from a strong concurrence-seeking tendency, the motivation for which is to maintain the friendly intragroup relations of a cohesive group. This tendency leads to support for the majority's preferred alternative at the cost of examining the other options; no effort is made to explore other courses of action and a selective bias rejects information that does not support the chosen path. The symptoms of groupthink were displayed in the seriously flawed logic underlying the policy-making of the Kennedy administration that resulted in the Bay of Pigs fiasco in 1961 (Janis 1972) and NASA's decision in 1986 to launch the space shuttle *Challenger* that ended in disaster (Moorhead *et al.* 1991).

In reviewing the literature on individual differences in accident liability, Lawton and Parker (1998) conclude that a multiperspective approach is necessary. The authors identify two routes by which

Chapter 5

Job stress and work-related accidents

The link between occupational stress and work-related accidents remains a much under-researched area. This chapter reviews the existing evidence. There are two major ways in which occupational stress affects work accidents: direct effects on workers' behaviour and indirect effects, mediated by employee health and well-being. Table 5.1 overviews the relationships between stress and accident involvement.

As previously suggested in Chapter 3, empirical studies have supported a mediation role for safety climate (workers' perceptions of the work environment), linking organisational factors to workers' behaviours (Neal *et al.* 2000; Griffin *et al.* 2002; Zohar 2002a; Barling *et al.* 2002). This represents one pathway by which organisational factors influence accidents, via the safety climate.

Neal *et al.* (2000) examined the effects of organisational climate on safety performance in an Australian hospital; they found a significant relationship mediated by safety climate. Organisational climate was measured in terms of employees' perceptions of different aspects of their work environment (appraisal and recognition, goal congruency, role clarity, supportive leadership, participative decision-making, professional growth, professional interaction) and safety climate in terms of employees' perceptions of management values, communication, training, and safety systems. The results suggest that the influence of general organisational climate is completely mediated by safety climate, as organisational climate did not contribute to performance, once the effects of safety climate had been partialled out.

A number of studies have found that aspects of leadership style are related to safety performance, mediated by safety climate. Zohar (2002a) found that leadership dimensions were significantly

Table 5.1 The effects of job stress on work accidents

Source	Effects on work accidents
Acute stressors (e.g. time pressure, noise, excessive workload)	Reduction in workers' capacities (e.g. slower reaction time, suboptimal decision making processes) and distractions increase the likelihood of errors; taking short cuts (violations) (temporary effects during stressful period).
Ongoing (chronic) stressors	Direct effects (e.g. lack of job clarity leads to working in unfamiliar situations) increase the likelihood of errors; indirect effects mediated by reduced mental and physical health (depression, anxiety, dissatisfaction, physical ill-health) lead to lowered capacity and motivation (long-term effects).
Stressful working environment leads to high absenteeism and staff shortages	Remaining staff experience increase in work pressure, leading to increased accident liability; violation promoting conditions.
Relationship between stress response and accident involvement is moderated by personality characteristics	Certain individuals (e.g. high Type A) are predisposed to perceive the work environment to be more stressful; these individuals have increased accident liability.
Stress mediates the relationship between personality and accidents	Certain individuals may actively position themselves in situations that expose them to a more stressful working environment; individuals will respond to stressors in different ways depending on their personality, leading to a further effect via coping strategies (which moderate the relationship between stress and accidents).
Social support has an indirect effect on accidents by buffering the individual against the effects of job stress	A lack of social support results in psychological strain, which in turn reduces capacity and increases accident liability (error-producing conditions); social support also has a direct effect on safe behaviour, by increasing safety motivation.

predictive of supervisory practices that were closely associated with them. Transformational leadership influenced open and informal communication between supervisors and subordinates, while corrective transactional leadership influenced the priority of production over safety. In both cases, the results suggested a complete mediation model, whereby leadership style predicted safety climate, which in turn predicted injury rate. Zohar concludes that the mediation effect of safety climate arises as supervisory practices that clarify real (as opposed to formally declared) priorities are reinforced. The study highlights that specific dimensions of leadership style are related to specific aspects of the safety climate. In another study examining leadership, Griffin *et al.* (2002) found that the relationship between local leadership and both safety participation and safety compliance was fully mediated by safety climate. Senior leadership was only partially mediated by safety climate. Safety-specific transformational leadership and role overload were related to occupational injuries through the effects of perceived safety climate (Barling *et al.* 2002).

Organisational factors may also influence work accidents by a second pathway mediated by occupational stress. Previous work has linked organisational climate with stress in relation to mental health outcomes, rather than workplace accidents. One study to examine work-related injuries was conducted by Hemingway and Smith (1999). They found that the relationship between organisational climate and work-related injuries was mediated by occupational stress.

Although links between perceptions of the work environment and stress responses would be expected, there has been little cross-reference between research conducted on occupational stress and the literature concerning safety climate. In a rare exception, a study by Morrow and Crum (1998) found that safety culture (climate) was a significant predictor of occupational stress. In multiple regression analysis, partialling out the effects of objective risk factors (including risk exposure, prior injury and tenure), safety culture was found to be a significant predictor of stress, such that a more positive safety culture was associated with lower stress. Safety culture was measured by an instrument developed specifically for the study (including nine items, e.g. 'safety is an important concern at [company name]'). Job stress was measured using a thirteen-item scale devised by Parker and DeCotiis (1983), including such items as 'my job gets to me more than it should'. The two variables were correlated significantly ($r = -0.38$, $p<0.01$). Safety culture was also a significant predictor of work-related attitudes, including work satisfaction, job involvement, organisational commitment and intention to stay. Morrow and Crum (1998: 310) note that: 'improved safety perceptions may have positive spillover effects on employee-related attitudes, perceptions and behaviours'.

Figure 5.1 Proposed causal model.

The relationship between safety climate and occupational stress is likely to be reciprocal, that is stress has an indirect effect on accidents mediated by safety climate (the experience of stress at work affects the way the employee perceives the working environment, leading to more negative safety attitudes and beliefs) and safety climate has an indirect effect on accidents mediated by occupational stress (the way the working environment is perceived by the employee will affect the experience of workplace factors as stressful).

Based on previous empirical studies, the model in Figure 5.1 is proposed. The model represents the direct effects of stress on accidents (via employees' safety-related behaviour), but it will also have effects mediated by employee health. At an organisational level, the effects of job stress on the organisation's workforce may include increased absenteeism, high turnover or lowered job performance, e.g. high absenteeism may lead to staff shortages increasing workload on remaining personnel, thus making errors more probable. At an individual level, reduced health and well-being will affect efficiency, motivation and error proneness. Even if individuals attend work when feeling ill or distressed, their performance will be reduced, leading to increased likelihood of errors, and feelings of resentment, possibly leading to violations.

Job stress and unsafe acts

Reason (1995) describes two pathways via which organisational factors may influence accidents: *latent failure pathway*, where organisational deficiencies have a direct influence on the system's defences, and *active failure pathway*, where organisational factors lead to violation-promoting and error-producing conditions in the workplace, increasing the likelihood of unsafe acts (leading to accidents). Reason (1995: 1,710) lists 'high workload, deficient tools and equipment, time pressure, fatigue, low morale and conflicts between organisational and workgroup norms' among the 'local conditions that promote the commission of errors and violations'. Parker et al. (1992) distinguish between error producing factors, which adversely affect information processing, and violation producing factors, which influence attitudes, beliefs and group norms. Error-producing factors include high workload, inadequate knowledge, ability or experience, poor interface design, inadequate supervision, change, stressful environment and mental state (fatigue, preoccupation, distraction, anxiety, etc.). Direct effects of stress on unsafe acts (errors and violations) are likely to occur as a result of error-producing conditions, such as high workload, stressful environment (high demands, low control) and mental state (e.g. fatigue, distraction, anxiety), and violation-promoting factors, such as low morale and time pressure. The distinction between errors and violations (introduced in Chapter 4) is reinforced in the traffic psychology literature. Using the Driver Behaviour Questionnaire, studies (e.g. Reason et al. 1990) have differentiated between errors, lapses and violations, where violations are significantly predictive of private car driver accidents. Later research has identified two types of violations: *ordinary*, which relate to deviating from safety rules (e.g. disregard speed limit) and *aggressive*, which involve interpersonal conflicts with other road users (e.g. sound horn to indicate annoyance with another road user). It is ordinary violations that are significantly associated with crash involvement for motorists, truck drivers and company car drivers (Sullman et al. 2002). Violations occur in a social context and involve motivational as well as cognitive factors; they bring perpetrators into areas of greater risk, where errors are less readily forgiven (Reason 1995).

Stress generated within the work environment may have a direct effect on work-related accidents by increasing the likelihood of certain errors and violations. Much research in this area has focused on the effects of acute stressors (such as time pressure, noise, threat and workload) on human performance. Steffy et al. (1986) developed a model of the relationship between stress and accidents in which stressors cause acute reactions (e.g. anxiety, fatigue) which have the effect of decreasing cognitive and performance capacities, such as reaction times and judgement, increasing the probability of errors. The increase in accident risk is temporary, as the elevation of the stress symptoms (e.g. anxiety) results in the return of the workers' capacities to normal levels (Murphy *et al.* 1986). A stressful environment may also act to distract the worker from the task, increasing likelihood of errors, encouraging suboptimal decision-making processes and promoting violations.

High levels of psychological stress (experience of unpleasant emotional states and high emotional arousal) lead to maladaptive decision-making (Janis and Mann 1977). For example, faulty decision-making resulted from the heightened tension experienced as a result of acute stress in the case of the shooting down of an Iranian airliner by the USS *Vincennes*. Ways of coping with psychological stress are characterised by different forms of ineffective information processing strategies (unconflicted adherence, unconflicted change, defensive avoidance and hypervigilance). Effective decision-making is characterised by vigilance:

- *unconflicted adherence*: ignoring information about risk of losses, continues in present course of action;
- *unconflicted change*: uncritically changes to a new course of action, ignoring consequences in terms of risk;
- *defensive avoidance*: identifies serious risks in both alternatives – three ways of coping through procrastination, shifting responsibility to another or rationalisation, only attending to positive aspects of possible solutions;
- *hypervigilance*: obsessed with serious risk of loss, vacillation between alternatives, rapid search for other options, characterised by reduced memory span and simplistic, repetitive thinking (a 'panic' reaction);
- *vigilance*: identifies and assesses risks, looks for relevant information and evaluates risks involved in alternatives before making a decision.

The effects of acute stressors are largely cognitive, influencing the way that individuals process information. However, chronic stressors, which will also affect cognitive processes, are likely to have more wide-ranging effects on motivation, attitudes and behaviour.

Errors

A number of studies have found that exposure to chronic (ongoing) occupational stress is related to increased accident risk (Cartwright *et al.* 1996; Greiner *et al.* 1998; Kirkcaldy *et al.* 1997; Trimpop *et al.* 2000) and occupational injuries (Hemingway and Smith 1999). Exposure to long-term stressors will result in psychological and physical symptoms of ill-health (e.g. depression, dissatisfaction and physical illness), these symptoms will then lead to lower performance and increased error proneness; certain stressors may also have direct effects (e.g. Hemingway and Smith 1999).

There is evidence to suggest that exposure to a stressful working environment has a direct effect on the ways that individuals process information. Hockey *et al.* (1996) suggest that stress directly affects performance by encouraging the use of short cuts in cognitive processing as a means of reducing mental effort. Reason (1990) argues that stress does not cause errors, however, it can lead to the adoption of certain cognitive styles that result both in higher rates of absentmindedness and inappropriate coping strategies. This may have ongoing effects as Broadbent *et al.* (1986) have demonstrated that high levels of self-reported cognitive failure are related to vulnerability to external stressors; trainee nurses with higher scores showed significantly higher levels of stress symptoms when working in more stressful environments. Long-term stress may also have an indirect effect via the psychological strain it causes, for example, Houston and Allt (1997), in a study of junior house officers, found that psychological distress was linked to significant medical errors, in addition to everyday errors. Melamed *et al.* (1989: 1,108) suggest that: 'preoccupation with disturbing job and work environment characteristics . . . is an important contributor to accident involvement. This preoccupation may serve as a distracting factor making the worker less attentive to danger cues'. This highlights the contribution of job stress to the type of mental state associated particularly with skill-based errors, i.e. preoccupation and distraction (see Chapter 4).

The experience of occupational stress in situations characterised by both excessive work demands and psychological distress is significantly associated with fatigue (Hardy *et al.* 1997). Rosa (1995) found excess fatigue, sleepiness and significant loss of sleep was characteristic of workers on extended work shift schedules (10–12 hour shifts). Moreover, within an extended shift, Rosa *et al.* (1989) found evidence of performance deficits, decreased reaction time and grammatical reasoning performance, and increased subjective fatigue after a seven-month period of 12-hour shift (relative to a previous shift pattern of 8 hours). This research evidence suggests that fatigue is a significant factor associated with work stressors, particularly high work demands and long hours, that results in reduced performance, and therefore increased likelihood of errors.

Violations

Violations are defined as 'deliberate infringements of safe working practice' (Reason 1993). The experience of stressors, e.g. time pressure, work overload, can encourage individuals to engage in violations, especially short cuts that provide quicker or more efficient ways of working. An understanding of why violations occur depends both on the organisational safety climate, and the subclimate associated with the employees' work group or department. The safety climate should encourage work behaviours that are safe and appropriate for the situation. This requires an understanding of the safety goals of the organisation, the assumption that safety takes a high priority and the knowledge, skills and confidence to accurately assess workplace hazards.

The definition of violations depends on how one defines 'safe' (e.g. do company rules always provide the safest way of working, or do employees sometimes know short cuts which are safer?). Defining violations in terms of 'deviations from a norm' widens the understanding of employee behaviour, as deviations can occur in relation to rules, standards or regulations; what is regarded as normal or usual; what is adequate or acceptable (Clarke 1994). For example, deviating from a company safety rule may also involve a deviation from what is acceptable (the practice is unsafe), but not from what is regarded as normal by the employee's work group (it is part of the work group's cultural norms). The safety climate will play an important role in determining the extent to which standard working practices (ways of working which are regarded as normal or usual) deviate from company rules (*normal violations*) (Clarke 1994). A high level of normal violations is often indicative of an unsatisfactory set of procedures. However, even where rules are largely appropriate, the operational procedures actually performed will always tend to differ from those prescribed in formal regulations to some extent (Wilpert and Klumb 1993). This is due to the operators' need to serve system operability, rather than a slavish adherence to company rules (and 'working to rule' can be successfully used as a form of industrial action). Normal violations are not unsafe in the eyes of the operator, but can lead to latent failure due to the insiduous accumulation of small failures over time. However, *anomalous violations* (Clarke 1994) are not appropriate behaviours (although they might serve a variety of purposes for the operator, e.g. saving time or effort, relieving boredom or testing skills), they are unacceptable and potentially unsafe. Clarke (1994) argues that anomalous violations must be understood at a group level, as these violations vary across locations, but normal violations are consistent within a category of workers.

Stressors will affect the commission of violations in two ways: first, by acting as violation promoting conditions, that is, a temporary effect in which the experience of stress (such as time pressure) will encourage the use of short cuts and the 'bending' of rules; and second, an effect mediated by the safety climate. Working within a positive safety climate will allow normal violations, which are necessary for system operability and are safe and appropriate under local conditions, but will give clear guidelines regarding the unacceptability of other types of rule violation. This is a climate which allows workers to assess the hazards within a particular situation and act accordingly, in the terminology of Reason *et al.* (1998), to allow *correct violations* (violating an inappropriate rule, due to an accurate hazard assessment) and discourage *mispliances* (rigid compliance with rules, where an accurate hazard assessment would suggest greater flexibility), but clearly forbid the violation of appropriate rules. The experience of acute stressors, such as excessive time pressure or work overload, can lead to supervisors turning a blind eye to the violation of appropriate rules, in order to reach production targets. Thus, acute stressors lead to a temporary adjustment of what is deemed acceptable, placing production over safety as the major priority. However, if high stress levels are experienced as the norm, rather than the exception, a permanent change in the nature of the safety climate can occur, such that employees develop negative attitudes and beliefs concerning safety, e.g. managers are perceived as lacking commitment to safety, employees have little ownership over safety issues, production takes priority over safety, etc. Thus, the negative influence of job stress is mediated by the safety climate. The damaging effects of a negative safety climate are likely to have long-term implications, as attitudes are translated into behavioural norms.

Job stress and safety behaviour

Employee behaviour influences safety performance, not only in terms of unsafe acts, but also in relation to a range of positive safety behaviours. Griffin and Neal (2000) identified two distinct components of safety-related performance: safety compliance and safety participation. *Safety compliance* involves adhering to safety procedures and carrying out work in a safe manner (relating to compliance with safety standards, rather than deviation from those standards, as discussed above). *Safety participation* involves helping co-workers, promoting safety within the workplace, demonstrating initiative, and putting effort into improving safety. Participation relates to safety-related organisational citizenship behaviours (or pro-role behaviours), including taking personal ownership of safety and reporting potential problems (Hofmann and Morgeson 1999) and the *propensity to actively care*, defined as 'acting to benefit the safety of other employees', e.g. reminding co-workers of hazards, confronting others about unsafe acts, picking up after others to maintain good housekeeping, correcting potential safety hazards where possible (Geller *et al.* 1996). Neal *et al.* (2000) found that perceptions of knowledge about safety and motivation to perform safely influenced individual reports of safety performance. The strongest effects related safety motivation, and to a lesser extent safety knowledge, to safety compliance, with weaker links between safety motivation and knowledge to safety participation. There was also a direct effect of safety climate on safety participation. This study highlights the particular importance of safety motivation in ensuring that employees adhere to safety rules and work in a safe manner. The role of safety knowledge in predicting safety performance is supported by Burke *et al.* (2002). This study found that depth of knowledge and skill was positively related to safety performance, but that breadth of knowledge was less important. However, the authors conclude that breadth of knowledge would have a stronger relationship to safety performance when the tasks are inconsistent in nature, such as non-routine tasks or emergencies, rather than general, routine tasks that are carried out in a more consistent manner (where depth of knowledge is required).

The development of behavioural norms in terms of the reporting of accidents, incidents and near-misses will depend on the safety climate. Clarke (1998a) found that the following reasons were significant predictors of train drivers' intentions not to report incidents: the incident was considered 'part of the day's work', managers would take no notice of reports, and the incident was routine and no action would be taken, even if it was reported. These results were indicative of a routinisation effect (whereby frequently encountered incidents were more likely not to be reported) and a reluctance to report based on anticipated (lack of) management response. Clarke (1998a) also found that the area where perceptions of managers were most negative had significantly lower intentions to report incidents compared to another two areas where more positive perceptions were held. The failure to report incidents is indicative of a safety climate in which managers are perceived as being unresponsive to safety information.

Geller *et al.* (1996) found that the propensity to actively care was significantly predicted by psychological reactance, personal control, group cohesion and extraversion at two industrial sites. People who were more willing to actively care, had a greater sense of belonging within the group, felt more empowered and were more extraverted; regarding the negative predictive power of psychological reactance, Geller *et al.* (1996: 7) suggest that 'given a top-down, rule-enforcement perception of corporate safety, it seems reasonable that persons scoring high on reactance would be relatively unwilling to go beyond the call of duty and actively care for the safety of other employees'. This research would suggest that the encouragement of pro-role safety behaviour will depend on a safety climate characterised by a sense of belonging and empowerment; a safety climate that alienates people through top-down policy enforcement will discourage such behaviours. Social support among co-workers (reflected by high scores on group cohesion) is also likely to support the development of pro-role behaviour within groups. Turner (1991) defines safety culture fundamentally as needing 'a genuine commitment from top management to a climate in which managers and employees can show that they *care* for the consequences of their actions, both for people and for things'; he adds that the authority to make changes is necessary to activate this care (Turner 1994).

As noted previously, the relationship between safety climate and occupational stress is likely to be reciprocal one. Morrow and Crum (1998) suggest the positive safety attitudes will spill over to other work-related variables, including job stress, such that a positive safety climate is predictive of reduced job stress. Post-hoc analyses conducted by Morrow and Crum (1998) indicated that safety importance interacted significantly with safety culture to explain additional variation in stress, that is the relationship between safety culture and stress was moderated by the importance attached to safety by the individual. Thus, it is important that the individual feels personal responsibility and ownership of safety, in order to reduce feelings of stress in the workplace. However, the experience of high levels of stress are also likely to affect the safety climate, fostering negative perceptions of management commitment, dissatisfaction with safety and reduced feelings of individual responsibility for safety. Working in a negative safety climate will reduce employees' willingness to participate in safety activities, including pro-role behaviour and reporting incidents, by reducing safety motivation and feelings of personal responsibility for safety.

Individual differences

It has been suggested that because individuals differ in their reactions to stress, that individual differences will play an important role in the effect of job stress on accident risk (Sutherland and Cooper 1991; Lawton and Parker 1998).

Bolger and Zuckerman (1995) suggest that personality may play an important role in the stress process by influencing individuals' exposure to stressful events (*differential exposure*), which then leads to outcomes, such as accidents; the relationship between personality and accident involvement is mediated by stress. For example, individuals high on Type A behaviour pattern may actively position themselves in situations that require ambition, drive and competitive behaviour, and therefore expose themselves to a more stressful working environment. This hypothesis has been the subject of little research in studies of job stress.

However, there is some evidence to support the differential exposure hypothesis in terms of accident involvement. People with different personalities seek out different types of jobs: Sutherland and Cooper (1991) found that a high proportion of extraverts worked on drilling rigs (most hazardous area of offshore oil platforms), while Farmer (1984) found that pilots are more aggressive and dominant than the norm. Different jobs have different safety characteristics, requiring different skills and abilities, e.g. where vigilance is required (such as air traffic control) errors are most likely to result in accidents, whereas a well-defended system is most at risk from violation of safe working practices (Lawton and Parker 1998), suggesting that individual differences will be important in determining how individuals will perform in varying work environ-ments. The work of Sherry (1991) on person–environment (PE) fit has suggested that a poor PE fit is related to accidents; a poor PE fit is likely to result in direct effects on individuals' behaviour, but also indirect effects, as greater stress will lead to the increased likelihood of accidents.

The alternative view (which is more investigated in the literature) is the *differential reactivity* hypothesis, that certain dispositional variables may moderate the impact of job stressors on employee outcomes. There are several mechanisms by which personality may moderate the effects of stress, including the effect that personality has on individuals' appraisals of situations (Cohen and Edwards 1989) and their choice of coping strategies.

Sutherland and Cooper (1991) concluded that certain personality characteristics (e.g. Type A behaviour) predispose some individuals to perceive the work environment to be more stressful and to be more accident involved. Furthermore, individuals will respond to experienced stress in different ways depending on their personality, leading to a further effect via coping strategies (which moderate the relationship between stress and accidents). Empirical work by Matthews and colleagues (e.g. Matthews *et al.* 1996, 1998) demonstrates that drivers' stress responses increase accident risk on the road. An aggressive response to driver stress was most predictive of increased accident involvement (Matthews *et al.* 1998). Aggressive driving predicted more frequent and more error-prone overtaking, behaviour that is related to the increased use of confrontational coping strategies in interaction with other vehicles (Matthews *et al.* 1998).

Evidence supports the role of a number of personality character-istics as moderating the stress–strain relationship, including Type A behaviour pattern, negative affectivity, self-esteem and locus of control. These individual differences are discussed in relation to work accidents in the following sections.

Type A behaviour pattern

There is evidence to suggest that individuals who demonstrate high Type A behaviour pattern (TABP) are more accident involved (Perry 1986; Evans *et al.* 1987; Sutherland and Cooper 1991; Magnavita *et al.* 1997), although West *et al.* (1993) found that TABP was associ-ated with faster driving, but not accident risk.

Two questionnaire measures, the Jenkins Activity Survey (Jenkins *et al.* 1971) and the Bortner Rating Scale (Bortner 1969), have been developed (see Table 5.2).

Both have been associated with accident involvement. Perry (1986) found significant simple correlations between scores on the Jenkins Activity Survey and number of accidents (0.29) and violations (0.35) and a questionnaire measure of driving impatience in a sample of fifty-four students. However, no account was taken of risk exposure, age or sex. A study of bus drivers in the United States and India using the Bortner Rating Scale (Evans *et al.* 1987) found that drivers characterised as Type A in both countries had higher accident rates than those characterised as Type B (the opposite pattern of behaviour), and that for the Indian sample Type A

Table 5.2 Example of a measure of Type A behaviour based on the Bortner Rating Scale

Style of Type B behaviour	Style of Type A behaviour
Casual about appointments	Never late
Not competitive	Very competitive
Good listener	Anticipates what others are going to say, nods and attempts to finish
Never feels rushed, even when under pressure	Always rushed
Can wait patiently	Impatient while waiting
Takes things one thing at a time	Tries to do many things at once, thinks about what will do next
Slow, deliberate talker	Emphatic in speech, fast and forceful
Cares about satisfying oneself, no matter what	Wants a good job recognised by others
Slow doing things	Fast eating, walking, etc.
Easy-going	Hard-driving, pushing oneself and others
Expresses feelings	Hides feelings
Many outside interests	Few interests outside home/work
Unambitious	Ambitious
Casual	Eager to get things done

Source: adapted from Sutherland and Cooper (2003).

personality was associated with more frequent braking, passing and use of the horn. Sutherland and Cooper (1991) found that TABP (high need for achievement, hard driving, competitiveness, impatience and time urgency) was associated with significantly more accidents, greater job dissatisfaction, poorer levels of psychological well-being and higher levels of stress. The concept of a Type A behaviour pattern has come under criticism recently. It has been suggested that it may cover two or more underlying dimensions which are canvassed to differing degrees by different measures; the Bortner Scale, for example, appears to factor into one dimension of competitiveness and one of speed (Edwards *et al.* 1990).

TABP is characterised as displaying very high levels of concentration and alertness, achievement striving, competitiveness, time urgency and aggressiveness on one hand, and irritability, hostility and anger, on the other. There is some support for TABP as a moderator of the stressor–strain relationship (Moyle and Parkes 1999; Payne 1988) but other studies demonstrate little support (Burke 1988; Edwards *et al.* 1990; Jamal 1999). Ganster *et al.* (1991) suggest that individuals who display anger/hostility toward people may be more prone to the adverse consequences of stressful work conditions (compared to TABP individuals who are low on this dimension), as only this dimension, not TABP as a whole, was related to physiological outcomes. Similar results were found using the Jenkins Activity Survey, where the anger/hostility dimension was associated with physical illness (Lee *et al.* 1993). George (1992) argues that TABP is not associated with psychological strain or distress, but that there is evidence to suggest greater risk of physical health problems.

It is possible that greater accident involvement is associated with TABP in individuals who display anger/hostility, as these individuals are more likely to express aggression (general anger is predictive of anger as a response to impeded progress on the road, which is predictive of an aggressive response: Lajunen and Parker 2001). TABP would be related to accidents due to an increased propensity for violations, such as speeding. This is supported by West *et al.* (1993), who found that TABP was significantly predictive of driving speed, and Perry (1986), who found a significant relationship between TABP and violations. However, much of the research relating to TABP is conducted within a road traffic environment; further research is needed to replicate these findings in a work context.

Choice of coping strategies may influence the impact of high TABP on accident involvement, e.g. one may cope with work overload by working overtime, increasing fatigue and increasing the likelihood of an accident. Some stressors may be self-created, e.g. an abrasive personality can create interpersonal conflicts.

Negative affectivity/neuroticism

The evidence linking neuroticism (a common measure of negative affectivity) to accident involvement was discussed in Chapter 4. The tendency to experience negative emotions (negative affectivity) has a significant positive relationship with occupational injuries (Iverson and Erwin 1997). The authors suggest that not only are neurotics more distractible, but also they prefer less direct coping strategies, such as emotion-focused coping (Parkes 1990), increasing their accident risk. Neuroticism was the strongest single predictor of driver stress (Matthews *et al.* 1991), suggesting that neurotics may respond more negatively to the presence of stressors, increasing their vulnerability to accidents. This is supported by Sutherland and Cooper (1991), who examined neuroticism in offshore oil workers: high neurotics were involved in significantly more accidents, and were also more dissatisfied, reported lower mental health and were more likely to be heavy drinkers when onshore.

Negative affectivity (NA) reflects a relatively stable pre-disposition to experience low self-esteem and negative emotional states (Watson and Clark 1984). It may act as a 'vulnerability' factor as high NA individuals are more susceptible to the effects of stress-inducing environments (Parkes 1990). Spector *et al.* (2000) outline six mechanisms for the effects of NA in the stressor–strain relationship. There is some evidence to be found in the literature to support each mechanism, suggesting that NA does not have a simple relationship within the stress process.

- NA directly affects perceptions of stressors (high NA have a 'negative world view'): *symptom perception*. High NA individuals were found to report significantly higher levels of eight out of nine stressors, higher job dissatisfaction and poorer levels of mental health (Sutherland and Cooper 1991).
- NA more sensitive to the impact of stressors, therefore NA has a direct effect on strain: *hyper-responsivity*. Neuroticism was

the strongest single predictor of driver stress (Matthews *et al.* 1991), suggesting that neurotics may respond more negatively to the presence of stressors, increasing their vulnerability to accidents.

• High NA individuals are more likely to be found in jobs that are 'stressful' (low autonomy and job scope): *differential selection.* Sutherland and Cooper (1991) expected that neurotic individuals would prefer a non-stimulating environment and would be employed on the production platform, rather than drilling, however, significantly more high NA individuals were found on the drilling rigs (more 'stressful').

• Behaviour of high NA individuals gives rise to stress, particularly by creating conflict and difficult social environment: *stress creation.*

• NA is an outcome of mood, affected by job conditions: *transitory mood.*

• Consistent exposure to stress induces high NA: *causality.*

There is evidence to suggest that each of the first three explanations could account for the relationship between NA and accident involvement. In addition, high NA is associated with the use of relatively ineffective coping strategies (Dorn and Matthews 1992; Iverson and Erwin 1997; Sutherland and Cooper 1991).

Locus of control

There is tentative evidence that locus of control (LOC) has a buffering effect on the stressor–strain relationship (Cohen and Edwards 1989), although Semmer (1996) suggests that the evidence in occupational settings is mixed. However, there is only limited support of an effect of external locus of control on accident involvement (such that 'externals' feel they have less control over events and their personal circumstances than 'internals'), given that any effects are generally fairly small (see Box 5.1).

Using the Safety Locus of Control Scale, Jones and Wuebker (1993) found that externals have more accidents than internals. However, studies using the Rotter Scale have found that internals have more accidents (Mayer and Treat 1977; Sims *et al.* 1984) or that there is little relationship (Janzen 1983; Guastello and Guastello 1986). Looking at self-reported traffic accidents, Clement and Jonah (1984) found that male externals reported more accidents,

---

Box 5.1   Example of a measure of locus of control based on the
Rotter Scale

1   Our society is run by a few people with enormous power
and there is not much the ordinary person can do about it
2   One's success is determined by 'being in the right place at
the right time'
3   There will always be industrial relations disputes no
matter how hard people try to prevent them or the extent
to which they try to take an active role in union activities
4   Politicians are inherently self-interested and inflexible – it
is impossible to change the course of politics.
5   What happens in life is predestined
6   People are inherently lazy, so there is no point in spending
too much time in changing them
7   I do not see a direct connection between the way and how
hard I work and the assessments of my performance that
others arrive at
8   Leadership qualities are primarily inherited
9   I am fairly certain that luck and chance play a crucial role
in life
10   Even though some people try to control events by taking
part in political and social affairs, in reality most of us are
subject to forces we can neither comprehend nor control

Greater agreement = more external locus of control
Lesser agreement = more internal locus of control

Source: adapted from Watts and Cooper (1998).

---

but that for females internals reported more accidents (quite small
effects).

A meta-analysis of traffic accidents (Arthur *et al.* 1991) suggested
a small-moderate effect for external locus of control. This would
suggest that individuals who perceive that accidents happen due to
forces outside their control (external locus of control) are less likely
to take personal responsibility for safety or take precautions to
prevent accidents occurring. An internal locus of control could also

influence accident involvement by buffering the individual from the negative consequences of stressors, protecting employee health and well-being, thus reducing accident vulnerability.

Self-esteem

Individuals with low self-esteem are more reactive to adverse conditions as they react more to external cues; they experience uncertainty about the correctness of their thoughts and emotional reactions, seek social approval and tend to be more self-critical; they also use more passive coping strategies (Ganster and Schaubroeck 1995). The evidence of self-esteem acting as a buffer against negative effects of stressors is supportive (Cooper *et al.* 2001). There are a few empirical studies linking self-esteem to road traffic accidents, but little in relation to work accidents. Norris *et al.* (2000) found that lower self-esteem was significantly associated with more traffic accidents; a similar finding was reported by Smith and Heckert (1998). However, in a sample of young male drivers, there was a significant relationship between high self-esteem and accidents (Vavrik 1997); in the particular subgroup examined, male adolescents may use risky driving as a way of showing off and increasing self-esteem.

The relationship between low self-esteem and road accidents may reflect the *dislike of driving* (DIS) dimension of driver stress (Gulian *et al.* 1989). In general, driver stress outcomes may result from appraisals that the demands of driving exceed or tax the person's ability to cope with those demands. The DIS dimension reflects the individual's negative appraisals of personal competence as a driver. This aspect of driver stress would relate to people who are low in self-esteem, as these individuals regard failure as 'self-diagnostic' and thus more stressful (Brockner 1988), affecting the way that they appraise situations. In terms of driving behaviour, individuals who score high on DIS perceive themselves as low in skill and judgement, and tend to adopt emotion-focused coping strategies, which generate worries that can interfere with vehicle control, thus increasing their accident potential (Matthews 1993). In contrast, some individuals may gain self-esteem from driving (Vavrik 1997) through risky and aggressive driving. This may relate to a further dimension of driver stress, driving aggression, which may be associated with negative appraisals of other drivers as hostile and threatening. This leads to the adoption of confrontive coping strategies, which generate risky and dangerous behaviours, increasing accident risk.

Coping strategies

In a review of the literature, Kinicki *et al.* (1996) found that both environmental and personality factors influence the choice of coping strategies, but that relationships between coping strategies and outcomes are inconsistent and moderating effects not always found. Cooper *et al.* (2001) note that dispositional coping style is likely to moderate the influence of environmental factors (stressors) on outcomes (strain), whereas coping behaviours mediate the effect of stressors on strain (coping with high workload by working harder reduces strain associated with the initial demands). Harris (1991) suggests that the range of coping strategies available is to some extent determined by organisational values, culture and norms; organisational factors can influence both primary appraisal (meaning of a particular encounter) and secondary appraisal (availability of coping resources). Ferguson and Cox (1997) classify the functions of coping strategies as: emotional regulation, approach, reappraisal and avoidance. Both problem-focused and emotion-focused coping strategies can be successful (effective), depending on the situation and how it is appraised by the individual (Erera-Weatherley 1996).

Much of the evidence related to accident involvement highlights the negative effects of emotion-focused coping strategies. The previous discussion has identified certain personality characteristics, including TABP, neuroticism and low self-esteem, as predisposing individuals to choose more passive, emotion-focused coping strategies. The use of these ways of coping is likely to be less effective in many situations, leading to continued stress, and increased accident vulnerability. There can also be long-term deleterious effects, both in terms of employee health and safety implications, where emotion-focused coping leads to heavy drinking, smoking or drug use. In a review of the literature, Stallones and Kraus (1993) estimate that for work accidents involving motorised vehicles up to 27 per cent involve a positive BAC (blood alcohol concentration). This evidence suggests that excessive alcohol use plays a significant role in approximately one in four work-related road fatalities. Although there is some evidence that cannabis use is associated with greater accident involvement (Crouch *et al.* 1989), there is a lack of reliable empirical research on drug use and work accidents (Guppy and Marsden 1996).

Summary

This chapter has discussed the mechanisms by which stress influences accident involvement. It is evident that stressors, both acute and chronic in nature, have a significant effect on accident involvement, either directly affecting employees' behaviour (unsafe acts and safety behaviours) or indirectly via psychological and physical strain. However, Brief and George (1991) warn against conceptualising the stress process as occurring at an individual level. While certain individuals may be identified as being 'high risk' in terms of accident vulnerability, it is clear that stressors in the working environment present significant risks in terms of work accidents. Any approach to risk assessment and risk reduction must focus both on the identification of vulnerable individuals and the remediation of risk factors for the workforce as a whole. It is also noted by Sparks *et al.* (2001) that many research investigations and workplace interventions for employee well-being are conducted at the managerial level, frequently excluding more subordinate employees (e.g. Neck and Cooper 2000; Worrall and Cooper 1998). Yet, in terms of work-related accidents, these individuals are usually in the frontline, and most likely to suffer the adverse effects of workplace accidents, although work-related accidents (such as car accidents) will also affect managerial staff. Accident involvement should not be thought to reflect contribution to accident causation, as managers will contribute to accidents through inadequate decision-making, as a result of work stress. However, these are latent, rather than active failures, as the adverse effects of managerial actions are not always immediately apparent (Reason 1990).

Chapter 6

A risk management approach to occupational stress

The previous chapter discussed the association between stress and occupational safety, emphasising that workplace stressors, both acute and chronic in nature, have a significant effect on work accidents. Much of the research has focused on the direct effects of acute stressors, which increase workers' error proneness. However, the evidence suggests that chronic stressors will have both direct effects on employees' behaviour (unsafe acts and safety behaviours), and indirect effects mediated by employee health and well-being. Stress management programmes aimed at the reduction of occupational stress are likely to have wide-ranging effects, both in terms of the improvement of employee health, and in terms of behavioural outcomes, including work accidents, absenteeism and productivity. Empirical evidence suggests that workplace interventions can be successful in reducing the experience of stress (Cooper *et al.* 1996; Murphy 1988) and negative behavioural outcomes, such as absenteeism and productivity (Berridge *et al.* 1997; Brulin and Nilsson 1994; Terra 1995). In a review of stress intervention practices for the European Commission (Cooper *et al.* 1996), examples of significant cost benefits over and above implementation costs are reported, illustrating the financial benefits of stress reduction programmes for organisations.

However, stress interventions are often applied as isolated measures, rather than being part of an integrated approach to organisational health. There is some evidence that the beneficial effects of stress management programmes are relatively short lived (Cooper *et al.* 1996). This may result from an overemphasis on the individual, particularly the tendency of stress management interventions to focus on reducing the effects, rather than reducing the presence, of stressors at work (Kahn and Byosiere 1992).

Furthermore, systematic risk assessment is often lacking in the practice of stress prevention (Kahn and Byosiere 1992; Kompier *et al.* 1998). *Risk assessment* is a process employed widely by organisations, particularly as part of the effort to identify, evaluate and control the potentially harmful effects of physical hazards. However, there is increasing awareness that psychosocial hazards pose a significant danger, which also needs to be evaluated and controlled. Effective stress management should form part of a broader risk management process that involves three stages:

- hazard identification and assessment;
- risk evaluation (assessment of risk factors; design of risk control strategies);
- risk reduction (implementation of control strategies, monitoring and review).

The final chapters of this book are devoted to a discussion of each of these three risk management stages. This chapter discusses the nature of risk management in this context, and describes a model that can be used for the management of safety risks related to occupational stress.

The concept of risk assessment

A *risk* can be conceptualised as having two basic elements, one relating to the chance (or probability) that an event, decision or activity will have undesirable negative outcomes, and the other relating to the severity of those outcomes. For example, Lowrance (1976) defines risk as 'a measure of the probability and severity of adverse effects'. More recently, a study group of the Royal Society (1983) ventured a more precise definition as 'the probability that a particular adverse event occurs during a stated period of time, or results from a particular challenge'.

Risk assessment has been defined as a 'process of estimating the probability and size of possible outcomes, and then evaluating the alternative courses of action' (Wharton 1992). This is commonly expressed within industry by the following equation (Ballard 1992):

$$\text{risk} = \text{frequency} \times \text{consequence}$$

Once an estimate of the level of risk has been obtained, a judgement must be made concerning the *acceptability* of that risk. Given the above equation, events with severe consequences must be very rare, and very frequent events must have low consequences. Frequent events with severe consequences represent an 'unacceptable' risk. In an example cited by Waring (1996), a manufacturing plant identified the use of ethoxol as a hazard (this is a respiratory irritant and narcotic); the frequency of exposure was high as it is airborne and levels varied between areas of the plant, the consequences were also high as the UK HSE has set maximum exposure limits which were exceeded in some areas. Using this simple formula, the risk would be assessed as unacceptably high and, if ethoxol could not be eliminated from the manufacturing process, risk control measures would have to be implemented to reduce exposure, e.g. changes in handling procedures or a 'no smoking/no eating' ban introduced.

Alternative formulae for evaluating risk have been suggested, e.g. Waring (1996) proposes that risk be related to the probability of a specific event (cf. Royal Society 1983 definition):

risk = consequences × exposure × probability (of an accident)

This equation might be applied to estimating the risk of a fire hazard in underground train stations. An identified hazard (people throwing down lighted matches or cigarettes and starting a fire) can be assessed as exposure (often) × consequences (minor) × probability (very unlikely), i.e. an acceptable risk. A more sophisticated approach might make use of technical information, e.g. incorporating equipment reliability data, such as the probability of water fog equipment failing. However, Toft (1993) argues that even for the assessment of major hazards, quantified risk assessments, which fail to take 'soft' factors into account, may be unsuitable. The validity of this argument is illustrated by re-evaluating the previous assessment in the light of a subsequent accident, such as at King's Cross in 1987, a disaster involving a serious fire in one of London's major underground train stations, which cost the lives of thirty-one people. The consequences might have been assessed as 'minor' as previous incidents had resulted in fires, but these were small scale and had resulted in few injuries and no loss of life; however, this demonstrates a misunderstanding of the available data, that is no serious injuries/fatalities to date does not imply potential low consequences. In terms of the probability of an accident, dropping a lighted match actually had a much higher chance of starting a serious fire due to the built-up debris under wooden escalators, which was not taken into account by technical estimates of the flammability of the escalators. Thus, although risk assessments may draw on objective and quantitative data, subjective judgement is often necessary in order to account for the human element in a system.

The above example illustrates how a fairly simple estimate of risk can be obtained for physical hazards, based on exposure (frequency × duration), consequences (injuries/fatalities) and probability of an accident. However, it must be appreciated that an over-reliance on 'objective' risk estimates, based largely on technical data, can be unwarranted. Cox and Cox (1993) differentiate between acute exposure (hazardous events) and chronic exposure (hazardous situations). In the latter case, the probability of a specific event (the accident) is less obvious as hazardous situations lead to *slow accidents*, that is the adverse effects of a hazard are delayed and are not immediately obvious. Yet it may be argued that many major disasters are 'slow accidents' as they have resulted from the accumulation of small failures over time (Turner 1978). In the above scenario, the fire hazard (dropping lighted matches) would best be understood as a trigger of a set of latent failures (built-up debris under the escalators, lax fire procedures, etc.) within the system (Reason 1990). The risk posed by chronic stressors might be evaluated in a similar way, e.g. as a mental or physical breakdown resulting from an accumulation of stress responses over time, akin to the 'slow accident'.

Risk assessment methodologies

Reviews of stress interventions have highlighted the key factors associated with a successful approach to stress prevention and control (Kompier 1996; Kompier *et al.* 1998). Kompier (1996: 362) emphasises the need for a 'participatory and stepwise' process, which includes the following stages:

- *preparation*: commitment from all parties, budget, plan, assessment of the cost of stress;
- *problem analysis (risk assessment)*: questionnaires, interviews, checklists; identify 'at risk' groups (e.g. older workers);
- *choice of measures*: tailor-made programme, link with other developments, consider impact across the company, avoid concentration on single stressors or partial solutions;

- *implementation*: change agents/organisational change, commitment and participation from all parties;
- *evaluation*: including a cost-benefit analysis.

Kompier *et al.* (1998) reviewed stress interventions conducted in ten Dutch companies. This review focused on five factors that characterised a successful approach: stepwise and systematic; adequate problem analysis; combination of measures aimed at both the individual and the work environment; worker participation; top management support. These reviews highlight the need for commitment from all parties (including the workforce and senior management) throughout the process, but particularly at the beginning (preparation) and at the implementation stage. Adequate problem analysis (or risk assessment) also emerges as a key stage, including a need to choose valid and reliable means of measuring stress (e.g. questionnaires, checklists, interviews).

Cox and Griffiths (1996) suggest that risk assessment methods fall into two categories: research design and epidemiology and practical 'case' assessments. Although the former methodology may be more scientifically rigorous, Cox and Griffiths argue that the latter approach is more pragmatic and concerned with risk reduction in specific situations or 'cases'. In such circumstances, a more practical, individual case methodology is appropriate, provided that it is based on

- adequate theoretical framework
- reliable and valid measuring instruments
- standard implementation procedures
- adequate data analysis.

Cox *et al.* (2000) argue that much of the research on stress prevention has limitations in terms of risk assessment. There are problems with sample selection or definition, data is handled at an individual level or the data produced is not easily interpreted in terms of risk reduction. There has been a tendency within stress research to focus on communalities across work groups, frequently neglecting differences between work groups and occupational differences (Sparks and Cooper 1999). Such an approach is difficult to reconcile with the practical need to develop group-specific solutions. Thus, a risk assessment methodology should focus on specific occupational groups, with an emphasis on identifying risk factors for that group.

Research conducted by Cox *et al.* (2000) on the risk management of psychosocial hazards emphasised the process of *translation*, which occurs during the interpretation of assessment data and the design of risk control measures. This process was identified as a complex and important stage in the overall risk management model. In addition to evaluating feedback from the assessment, translation involves the identification of 'underlying pathologies', dealing with the emotional reactions of all parties, and working through the ramifications of the risk control strategy, particularly the political implications. The research emphasised the need for political sensitivity and risk control strategies that can be integrated with ongoing corporate initiatives, with the minimum number of actions to address the maximum number of risk factors. The success of tailor-made stress prevention programmes is also noted by Kompier (1996), where programmes link with other developments, consider the impact across the company and avoid concentration on single stressors or partial solutions.

The following model of risk management is proposed, based on the previous research:

Stage one: assessment of job stress

- preparation: commitment from all parties, budget, plan, assessment of the cost of stress
- identification of hazards
- assessment of the associated risks

Stage two: risk evaluation

- calculation of risk factors
- design of reasonably practicable control strategies
- identification of change agents, commitment and participation from all parties

Stage three: risk reduction

- implementation of control strategies
- monitoring and evaluation of effectiveness of control strategies (including cost-benefit analysis)
- feedback and reassessment of risk
- review of information needs and training needs of employees.

The first stage involves problem analysis using stress audit instruments (e.g. questionnaires, interviews and checklists) to identify hazards (sources of workplace stress) and assess the level of associated harm (e.g. measures of physical health, psychological strain, job satisfaction, lost work days, sickness absence, accidents and incidents). Kompier (1996) emphasises the need for preparation, especially participation from the workforce and visible commitment from senior management. The second stage utilises the data collected in stage one to conduct a risk assessment and evaluation. Risk factors are calculated to reflect the relationship between exposure to workplace stressors and the extent of the negative consequences that are likely to follow. The production of risk factors allows the prioritisation of risk control strategies. An intervention programme should be developed in consultation with the organisation, including senior management and representatives of the workforce. The final stage involves the implementation of the risk reduction strategies. The process of monitoring and review should be ongoing and feed back into the risk management process (Health and Safety Executive 1991). The degree of success can be gauged by repeating the stress audit. This process allows an evaluation of the extent to which the negative consequences of stress previously identified have been reduced. At this stage the continuing cost-effectiveness of the programme can be assessed.

Risk assessment of occupational stress

Ongoing workplace stressors can be viewed as representing a hazard, although not necessarily a physical one, and relating to chronic exposure, rather than acute. The effects of occupational stress might be compared to the 'slow accident', whereby constant exposure leads to negative outcomes over time. The risk posed by workplace stressors can be understood in relation to three elements: exposure, consequences and probability.

Exposure

It may be less relevant to measure the duration and frequency of a stressor than a physical hazard, e.g. a low-level radiation leak may occur infrequently (every four to twelve weeks) for a short period of time (less than ten minutes), but a stressor, such as working to tight deadlines, might be best described as a constant source of pressure. It is possible to gain an objective measure of exposure to radiation by calculating the number and duration of radiation leaks within a given period, however, exposure to stress is subjective, that is the extent to which the individual perceives a particular work characteristic, such as working to deadlines, as a source of pressure will vary between individuals. Exposure can be operationalised as the level of perceived pressure from a given stressor. This is a quantifiable, but subjective, measure of exposure. While it may be possible to obtain 'objective' measures of stressors, e.g. number of hours worked per week could be taken as measure of workload, this fails to account for the dispositional differences between individuals. The same number of work hours can have a more negative effect on one individual due to his or her negative disposition (high in NA) than another who perceives the work situation more positively. Thus, it is important that it is the *perceived* level of stress that is measured.

Consequences

From an earlier example, exposing a person to a respiratory irritant (ethoxol) over time has known and specific effects, in the short term, breathing difficulties, and in the long term, lung disease. The consequences of exposure to stress are more varied and affected by numerous factors; possible consequences include physiological (e.g. high blood pressure, chest pains), psychological (e.g. depression, anxiety, irritability) and behavioural (e.g. excessive drinking, smoking) symptoms. In the long term, these symptoms may result in physical (e.g. coronary heart disease) and/or psychological (e.g. mental breakdown) ill-health, and a range of behavioural outcomes, including absenteeism, loss of productivity and work accidents.

Attempting to assess the risk associated with a specific stressor (e.g. meeting tight deadlines) resulting in a specific negative outcome (e.g. mental breakdown) for a particular individual is probably unworkable, given the number of factors that must be known, e.g. genetic predisposition, family history, individual coping styles, support available from spouse, etc. However, it may be possible to gain an understanding of the risk involved for a particular workforce with an identifiable negative outcome at an organisational level, e.g. sickness absence. Rather than focusing on assessing the risk for each employee, aggregating across individuals will give an estimate of the likelihood of negative consequences for a workgroup, or the organisation as a whole. Although employers still have a duty to identify vulnerable individuals and subsections of the workforce (e.g. older workers).

Probability

It might make better sense to work with 'probability' rather than 'consequences' as the severity of harm dimension of risk, that is the likelihood of exposure to a particular type of stressor (e.g. workload) resulting in a negative outcome (e.g. sickness absence). Given the difficulties of working at an individual level, these can be calculated for a particular workforce, at a group or organisational level. This relationship might be represented, for a particular workforce, as the correlation between a stressor and a stress outcome, e.g. if a correlation of $r = 0.50$ is found between 'working to deadlines' and the number of lost work days per year, this may be interpreted as shared variance between the two variables of 25 per cent ($r^2 = 0.25$), i.e. a probability of 25 per cent or 1:4.

One disadvantage of using values of r to generate probabilities is that the r statistic does not represent non-linear relationships. While it may be a valid assumption that an increasing experience of stress will lead to an increase in the negative outcome (e.g. more lost working days) for most stressors, some will deviate from this simple linear relationship. For example, workload has a U-shaped relationship with symptoms, e.g. within a certain tolerance limit (the bottom of the U), workload will generate few stress symptoms; as workload falls into the range of underload, this will be experienced as increasingly stressful (first arm of the U); and as workload falls into the range of overload, this will also be experienced as increasingly stressful (second arm of the U). This might be tackled by looking at overload and underload as two separate variables.

Risk evaluation

Evaluation of the data obtained from the risk assessment involves a number of steps. This process includes the calculation of risk factors for the workforce as a whole, identification of 'high risk' groups and individuals, understanding the links between exposure and consequences, and an assessment of the acceptability of the risks identified.

Calculation of risk factors

It is proposed that the *risk factor* associated with the likely negative effects of a given stressor may be calculated using the following equation:

risk factor = exposure (E) × probability (P)

E – the perceived level of the stressor
P – likelihood of exposure to stressor resulting in negative outcome

A stress audit instrument, such as the Occupational Stress Indicator (OSI) (Cooper *et al.* 1988) or Pressure Management Indicator (PMI) (Williams and Cooper 1996) can be used to obtain E (the level of perceived stress). These instruments also include measures of some outcome variables (mental and physical well-being, job satisfaction) allowing the calculation of P (the correlation between the level of a stressor and a stress outcome) for a particular sample. Additional information on further stress outcomes, such as absenteeism or accidents, would have to be collected separately: objective data, such as sickness absence, work days lost through accident involvement, etc., might be obtained from employee records.

Worked example: assessing risk factors for employee health

McFarlane (1997) conducted a stress audit within a leading UK retail organisation. A sample of blue-collar workers (N = 66) completed the PMI and the General Health Questionnaire. The GHQ is a well-validated instrument that measures symptoms of mental ill-health (Goldberg 1978).

Table 6.1 shows the mean perceived levels of stress associated with the eight PMI stressors and the correlations with GHQ.

Table 6.1 Sample risk factors for the PMI stressors (means for blue-collar retail workers, N = 66)

Stressors	Mean	r	$r^2 \times 100$	Risk factor
Workload	9.85	0.090	0.81	8
Relationships	13.49	−0.080	0.64	9
Recognition	11.29	−0.098	0.96	11
Organisational climate	12.05	−0.057	0.32	4
Personal responsibility	11.08	0.162	2.62	29
Managerial role	8.06	0.167	2.79	22
Home–work balance	8.91	0.155	2.40	21
Daily hassles	11.42	−0.006	0.004	0.05

Positive correlations with GHQ indicate that a stressor is associated with an increased level of negative health symptoms.

$$\text{risk factor (sample)} = E_{(s)} \times P_{(s)}$$
$$= \text{level of stressor} \times \text{probability of negative outcome}$$

e.g. workload = mean PMI score of 9.85, $E_{(s)} = 9.85$ correlation (r) between workload and mental health = 0.09, $P_{(s)} = 0.81$ (where P is a percentage 0–100)

$$\text{risk factor (sample)} = 9.85 \times 0.81 = 8$$

This procedure yields risk factors for this particular sample of retail workers, indicating the risk of developing negative health symptoms as a result of working for the organisation. Table 6.1 shows that daily hassles poses a very low risk (close to zero), while the highest risk is posed by home–work balance. Although the level of 'daily hassles' ($E = 11.42$) is comparable to the perceived stress associated with 'personal responsibility' ($E = 11.08$), the latter poses a far greater risk in terms of mental ill-health. This arises as P (personal responsibility) is 2.62 compared to P (daily hassles) at 0.004, resulting in a much higher risk factor for personal responsibility (29) compared to daily hassles (0.05). This result would indicate that this particular sample of workers is successful in coping with daily hassles, but less successful in coping with personal responsibility. Note that the stressor with the highest value of E (relationships, $E = 26.97$) does not have the highest risk factor.

Risk acceptability

The worked example yielded a risk factor of 8 for workload. While this figure has some meaning by comparison to other stressors within the sample, it is difficult to evaluate the relative level of the risk for an organisation (i.e. is it a 'low' risk?) without reference to normative values. Thus, it is proposed that the acceptability of a risk factor be determined by comparison to industry norms. This allows the level of the risk to be compared to that obtained from similar organisations with similar operations. The decision as to the 'acceptability' of a risk is determined by considering the cost of lowering the risk level, against the benefits from a reduction in risk.

Worked example: evaluating risk factors for employee health

For illustrative purposes, Table 6.2 shows the normative values of the PMI for the general working population (N = 14,455) and hypothetical values of r for the correlations of this normative population between the stressors and GHQ.

Normative risk factors for an industry can be calculated, where the norm for exposure, $E_{(norm)}$, and for probability, $P_{(norm)}$, are known:

$$\text{risk factor (norm)} = E_{(norm)} \times P_{(norm)}$$

e.g. workload, norm PMI score of 12.46, $E_{(norm)} = 12.46$ correlation (r) between workload and GHQ = 0.05, $P_{(norm)} = 0.25$.

$$\text{risk factor (norm)} = 12.46 \times 0.25 = 3$$

Comparing the risk factor (sample) to the risk factor (norm) gives a company an indication of the extent of the risk in their own organisation: a low risk might be the industry average or below; moderate risk might be up to 1 SD above the average (in the worst 34 per cent) and a high risk might be 1 SD or more above the average (in the worst 16 per cent). This would assume that companies form a normal distribution of risk factor scores for the industry. These scores could be converted to standard scores (z-scores) for ease of interpretation: for a low risk, z is zero (the score is the same as the industry standard) or negative (a risk lower than the industry standard); for a moderate risk, z is between 0 and 1, and for a high risk, z is above 1 (see Table 6.3).

Table 6.2 Normative risk factors for the PMI stressors (means for general working population, N = 14,455)

Stressors	Mean	r	$r^2 \times 100$	Risk factor
Workload	12.46	0.05	0.25	3
Relationships	13.44	0.20	4.00	54
Recognition	13.13	0.10	1.00	13
Organisational climate	13.65	0.25	6.25	85
Personal responsibility	12.73	0.30	9.00	115
Managerial role	9.94	0.23	5.29	53
Home–work balance	9.87	0.24	5.76	57
Daily hassles	11.71	0.10	1.00	12

Table 6.3 Definition of high, moderate and low risks by comparison to industry norms

Risk category	z-score	Comparison to norm
Low	−1 or lower	top 16%
	between 0 and −1	top 34%
	zero	average
Moderate	between 0 and +1	bottom 34%
High	+1 or above	bottom 16%

While exposure norms already exist for a number of industries and occupations, a review of the available data would be needed to determine the normative values of *P*, for a range of negative outcomes. One such method might involve a meta-analysis of the relationships between stressors and outcome measures found across studies. Although much of this work remains to be done, an unpublished doctoral thesis (Cass 2003) conducted a meta-analysis involving 600 studies; the study found significant effect sizes for the relationship between health and supervisor support (0.169), job security (0.133) and working hours (0.068).

Some indicative figures can be illustrated from large-scale studies, such as Jones *et al.* (1997), which compared self-reported working conditions and lost working days due to illness reported in a UK household survey. This study found that the increased likelihood of time lost through illness, given these working conditions, as follows: 'lack of help and support from people in charge' (6 times); 'working to deadlines' (4½ times); 'too much work' (4½ times).

Individual differences

The relationship between a stressor and a stress outcome is influenced by a number of individual difference variables, including personality, coping strategies and social support. Cox *et al.* (2000) argue that the existence of individual differences does not negate the overall assessment exercise, as sources of stress correspond to 'likely risk factors'. In the current model, the vulnerability of a given sample is accounted for within the value of *P*: a higher value of *P*, where there are few moderating influences, and a lower value of *P*, where the value is moderated. A workforce that has a high vulnerability to stress will produce a higher P value and, therefore, a greater risk factor.

If moderating variables are measured within the stress audit, the relative effects can be quantified. The relationship between the stressor and the stress outcome is represented by a simple correlation, r. The relative influence of a moderator can be quantified by calculating the partial correlation: removing the effects of a variable and examining the remaining correlation effect. For example, removing the effect of external locus of control may reduce the correlation between workload and sickness absence, as individuals high in externality are more vulnerable to the effects of workload, and are more likely to take sick leave, than those who have a more internal locus of control.

Risk reduction

The final stage involves the implementation of the risk control strategy (including identifying relevant resources). An important aspect of risk reduction is evaluating the impact of the risk control measures, including the effectiveness of the programme in reducing/ preventing stress (e.g. redistribution of the stress audit) and assessing the reactions of the workforce to the programme (e.g. interviews with employees).

Risk control measures

Once risk levels have been determined, and prioritised in terms of industry standards, risk control measures can be devised to reduce the risk associated with a stressor. In the worked example, only workload emerges as a stressor that has a risk factor above the industry average. The likelihood of negative outcomes (symptoms of mental ill-health) in the sample workforce, resulting from workload, is about twice that found in the general working population on average. Thus, examining the workload of employees would be the first step in devising an appropriate risk control measure. This might involve improving time management skills, so that employees can better manage their existing workloads (individual focused programme), or reorganising schedules so that workload is reduced (work environment focused programme). Kompier *et al.* (1998) recommend that a combination of individual and work environment based control measures will be most successful.

Monitoring and feedback

The final stage of the risk management process involves monitoring the effects of risk control measures, and evaluating their effectiveness. A further stress audit can be used to monitor the levels of exposure and the effects on outcome measures. An unsuccessful intervention will make little difference to the relationship between the stressor and the stress outcome, while a successful one will moderate that effect.

For example, if the intervention involved improving organisational help and support to vulnerable employees, partialling out the effect of social support will give an indication of the extent to which it is buffering workers against the effects of stress. An effective intervention will result in more employees seeking social support from the organisation, increasing their resistance to stress, and therefore lowering the risk factor for the organisation.

Stress interventions

Interventions to deal with occupational stress usually fall into three types of action: *primary* (eliminating, reducing or altering stressors in the working situation); *secondary* (approaches designed to prevent employees who are already showing signs of stress from getting sick and to increase their coping capacity) and *tertiary* (treatment activities directed at those employees who show strong stress reactions and rehabilitation after sickness absence) (Cooper and Cartwright 1994; Kompier 1996).

Kompier (1996) identifies four types of prevention and intervention possibility:

- *primary prevention – work environment intervention*: changing job content, e.g. job enrichment, worker participation, career development activities, team building, social support, etc.;
- *secondary/tertiary prevention – work environment intervention*: measures directed at employees showing signs of stress, e.g. special work schedules;
- *primary prevention – individual/group intervention*: selection, pre-employment medical examination, health promotion and wellness programmes (e.g. corporate fitness programmes, relaxation training);
- *secondary/tertiary prevention – individual/group intervention*: measures directed at individuals with serious stress-related

problems, e.g. rehabilitation, post-traumatic stress counselling, relaxation and psychotherapy.

The secondary and tertiary levels of intervention by organisations are most common. These focus on the individual, either through programmes that encourage more healthy lifestyles, e.g. keep-fit centres on site, dietary advice, relaxation and exercise classes, or provide education on how to develop more effective stress management skills. Tertiary interventions act to mitigate the symptoms of stress on an individual, e.g. helping individuals to cope with their anxiety through relaxation and biofeedback. The positive effects of an improved lifestyle can feed back into the stress process by boosting individuals' resistance to stress. Secondary interventions operate by improving the coping strategies of individuals and/or by replacing maladaptive coping styles with more successful ones, thus making the workforce less vulnerable to stress. Such stress interventions will lower the risk factor, by reducing the value of P (a more stress resistant workforce will have a reduced likelihood of experiencing stress symptoms), rather than by affecting the value of E, exposure to stressors. Primary interventions focus on stressor reduction. For example, where the nature of the job is leading to stress, the task or the work environment might be subject to redesign; where the organisation's structure or climate is the source of stress, a more participative management style might be encouraged. These interventions reduce exposure to stressors, lowering the value of E, and therefore reducing the risk factor.

A more detailed follow-up can help to determine exactly what type of risk control measures are required, depending on the type of stressor. Moderate risks might be reduced to low risks by providing training or organisational support (reducing P), while a high risk might need to be tackled at an organisational level (reducing E). If E is very high, reducing the value of P may not be sufficient to reduce the overall value of the risk factor to an acceptable level, thus, organisational interventions must be aimed at reducing exposure. However, while some solutions may be relatively inexpensive, e.g. providing protective screens to protect bus drivers from the threat of physical violence, those aimed at changing the organisation's culture or structure may involve considerable effort and expense. Using a risk management strategy as advocated in this book, allows companies to evaluate the relative level of risk involved, before embarking on expensive organisational development programmes.

Summary

This chapter has introduced a risk management model for assessing the risks associated with occupational stress. The model comprises three stages: assessment of job stress; risk evaluation and risk reduction. Each stage of the model is discussed in detail, with reference to case studies, in the following chapters.

Chapter 7

Assessment of job stress

This chapter reviews existing stress audit tools, particularly those suitable for the assessment of stress levels among blue-collar workers, which could be used in the first step of the risk management process. It provides comparisons in terms of administration, interpretation and availability of validation and normative data. The chapter also presents a case study of the assessment of job stress, using stress audit methodology.

Stress audit tools

There have been a number of organisational or occupational stress risk assessment instruments over the years. Most of these have been used for research purposes only (Zalaquett and Wood 1997), with a growing number of them being converted into use as an organisational risk assessment tool. The most notable one, which has been translated into over twenty languages and used both as an occupational stress research instrument as well as a risk assessment measure in industry and the public sector, is the Occupational Stress Indicator (Cooper *et al.* 1988), and its later development, the Pressure Management Indicator (Williams and Cooper 1996).

Occupational Stress Indicator

The OSI was the gold standard measure that was designed for research purposes, that is, to provide the research community with a standardised measure that could be used throughout the world for cross-cultural and occupational comparisons. There have been hundreds of studies published using the OSI (Williams and Cooper 1997). Reliability and validity studies largely support the methodological rigour of the instrument. However, there are a number of problems associated with the use of the OSI as a stress audit measure: it was designed primarily for use in research on white-collar and managerial jobs; it is very long, with over 160 items; the coping subscales are not very reliable (which tends to be the case with most coping measures); it contains personality subscales. In other words, it was earmarked for particular groups of people and was not appropriate for a variety of occupations or levels, and contains subscales not necessary for organisational auditing or risk assessment (i.e. personality factors and coping scales). The scales include three strain or outcome measures: mental and physical health, and job satisfaction. It measures six stressor factors: factors intrinsic to the job, role factors, relationships at work, career and achievement, organisational structure and climate and the home–work interface. It also contains three individual or personality factors; coping strategies, Type A behaviour and locus of control. Given that the OSI has been used so extensively, there is a large database of studies to provide normative comparisons, for the general population and for specific occupational groups.

Pressure Management Indicator

The OSI was refined to produce the Pressure Management Indicator, which is essentially very similar to the OSI, but with fewer of the original items and the inclusion of a small number of new ones (Williams and Cooper 1996). The PMI is still reasonably long (120 items), contains primarily white-collar type items (most of which derived from the OSI) and does not have the research infrastructure or publication base of the OSI. It was re-factored into very similar factors to the OSI, but with different titles such as state of mind, resilience, drive, patience–impatience, etc. However, given that the bulk of the item bank came from the OSI, it is not very different, but the descriptors are probably more comprehensible for a business audience. Nevertheless, the underlying problems of length, orientation, lack of research output and items that were derived in the 1980s, remain.

ASSET

Cartwright and Cooper (2002) designed ASSET specifically as a stress audit tool to be used by industry, rather than as a research instrument. Previous measures, such as the OSI, have been developed for use with managerial and/or white-collar populations; however, ASSET is aimed at a wider organisational setting. It measures eight sources of stress (workplace stressors), physical health, psychological well-being and organisational commitment (see Box 7.1 for example items). The theoretical basis of the ASSET instrument has similar roots to the OSI, assuming a transactional perspective of the stress process. The links between workplace stressors and employee outcomes are illustrated in Figure 7.1. The assessment of job stress comprises thirty-seven items divided into eight subscales which are identified as follows:

- *work relationships*: poor or unsupportive relationships with colleagues and/or superiors, isolation (a perceived lack of adequate relationships) and unfair treatment;
- *work–life balance*: difficulty maintaining a satisfactory balance between work responsibilities and personal/home life; the demands of work have the potential to spill over and interfere with individuals' personal and home lives;
- *overload*: unmanageable workloads and time pressures;
- *job security*: job insecurity and job changes; the fear of job loss or obsolescence;
- *control*: lack of influence in the way in which work is organised and performed;
- *resources and communication*: to perform their job effectively, individuals need to feel they have the appropriate training, equipment and resources; they also need to feel that they are adequately informed and that they are valued;
- *pay and benefits*: the financial rewards that work brings are obviously important in that they determine the type of lifestyle that an individual can lead; they often influence an individual's feelings of self-worth and perception of his or her value to the organisation;
- *aspects of the job*: the fundamental nature of the job itself, including physical working conditions, type of tasks and the amount of satisfaction derived from the job itself.

The instrument is self-administered; it is quick and easy to complete, taking approximately fifteen minutes for respondents to fill in the questionnaire, either on paper, or using the computerised version.

Box 7.1 Example items from ASSET

Perceptions of your job

Work relationships
My boss behaves in an intimidating and bullying way towards me
I feel isolated at work, e.g. working on my own or lack of social support from others

Work–life balance
I work longer hours than I choose or want to
I work unsocial hours e.g. weekends, shift work, etc.

Overload
The technology in my job has overloaded me
I am set unrealistic deadlines

Job security
My job is insecure
My job is likely to change in the future

Control
I have little control over many aspects of my job
I am not involved in decisions affecting my job

Resources and communication
I do not feel I am informed about what is going on in this organisation
I am not adequately trained to do many aspects of my job

Aspects of the job
My physical working conditions are unpleasant (e.g. noisy, dirty, poorly designed)
My performance at work is closely monitored

Pay and benefits
My pay and benefits are not as good as other people doing the same or similar work

Attitudes towards your organisation

Perceived commitment of organisation to employee
I feel valued and trusted by the organisation

I enjoy working for this organisation to the extent that I am
  not actively seeking a job elsewhere
Commitment of employee to organisation
If necessary, I am prepared to put myself out for this organisation, e.g. by working long and/or unsocial hours.
If asked, I am prepared to take on more responsibility or tasks
  not in my job description

Your health
Physical health
Lack of appetite or overeating
Insomnia – sleep loss
Psychological well-being
Panic or anxiety attacks
Constant irritability

Source: Cartwright and Cooper (2002).

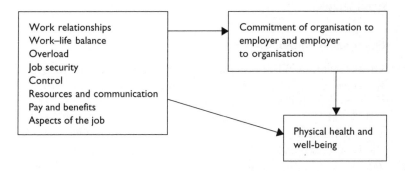

Figure 7.1 The ASSET model.
Source: adapted from Cartwright and Cooper (2002).

Analysis of the data allows comparison between groups within the
organisation (e.g. whether group A is more stressed than group B)
and against normative data (e.g. whether *neither* or *both* groups A
and B are more stressed than would be expected). Cartwright and
Cooper (2002) recommend that data comparison be undertaken at

both the scale and item level. Normative data are derived from a sample of 9,188 people from public and private sector organisations in the United Kingdom. Sten scores are quoted to indicate the level of the stressor against the normative data. These are standardised scores on a scale of 1–10, with a mean of 5.5 and standard deviation of 2. For example, the sten scores for levels of occupational stress:

- mean scores below sten 3 indicate very low levels of the stressor;
- mean scores below sten 4 indicate low levels of the stressor;
- mean scores within the range defined by sten 4 to sten 7 are 'average';
- mean scores above sten 7 indicate high levels of the stressor;
- mean scores above sten 8 indicate very high levels of the stressor.

ASSET has advantages in terms of ease of completion and being designed for blue-collar workers, but has (as yet) limited tests of reliability and validity (though data published by Robertson Cooper Ltd to date show these to be satisfactory). Limited use means that the normative data provided have been developed from a relatively small sample.

Other occupational stress measures

There are a number of other measures that could be used for stress auditing that were not designed for that purpose, which can be found in the book of resources entitled *Evaluating Stress* (Zalaquett and Wood 1997), but many of these are primarily research focused and not designed as a risk assessment or stress audit instrument. The UK Health and Safety Executive is developing its own risk assessment measure, which is likely to be similar to ASSET in terms of the organisational stressors, given that the research in this field has clearly identified a similar number of workplace sources of stress.

Differing approaches may be needed, depending on size of the organisation. For example, small businesses may benefit from the use of interviews with staff, rather than a survey. While standardised assessments (such as the OSI, PMI and ASSET) have the advantage of normative comparisons, tailor-made assessment surveys (based on interviews with personnel) can also be used (Cox *et al.* 2000). These can give a unique insight into the specific stressors identified by the particular occupational or work group.

Many of the instruments available are self-completion surveys, but require professional interpretation. Researchers have suggested that particular attention be paid to the development of methods and tools to assess workplace stress that can also be used by non-professionals in the workplace (Kompier and Levi 1993).

A case study is included (using ASSET) to illustrate the assessment of job stress as the first step of the risk management process (source: Joe Jordan, Robertson Cooper Ltd).

Case study: stress auditing at Somerset County Council

Introduction

In 2001–2 Robertson Cooper Ltd (RCL), the business psychology firm, undertook a major stress audit within Somerset County Council (Somerset CC) in south-west England. This case study highlights why Somerset CC undertook the audit, how the audit was delivered, some of the results of the audit, and the post-audit action planning that took place.

Local authorities in the United Kingdom are sensitive to the problem of workplace stress. They have borne the brunt of a rise in stress litigation and have provided much of the case law that exists in this area.

The UK HSE also recognise local authorities as employers of several 'high risk' employee stress categories: these include social workers and teachers.

Against this backdrop, Somerset CC wanted to explore ways in which it could proactively manage its approach towards employee stress. A stress audit is an important way in which to apply the HSE's principle of prevention specified in Regulation 3 of the Management of Health and Safety at Work Regulations 1999. An employer has to identify proactively causes of work-related stress, undertake effective risk assessment, and implement measures which, so far as is reasonably practicable, prevent or control the risk of psychological harm.

Survey methodology of the form used in the stress audit by Somerset CC not only deals with the identification of stressors, but also deals with other problems that organisations have when they try to deal with workplace stress problems:

- It provides benchmarking data so that the organisation can determine which parts of its business are most at risk.
- So long as a validated and standardised stress auditing instrument is used, it will provide external benchmarking so that the organisation can determine the magnitude of the risk by comparing its results with general population or sector specific data.
- It also overcomes some of the difficulties associated with a manager-dependent process where the identification of stress risks is left to the manager to identify and to deal with. This can be a big problem for organisations. Managers very often do not know how to undertake a proper stress risk assessment. Also, very often they have blind spots when it comes to recognising stress risks, preferring to sweep stress problems under the carpet rather than confronting them. And perhaps the biggest problem is that managers themselves can be the most pernicious of workplace stressors.

The results of a stress audit provide an evidence-based need for action.

Conducting a stress risk assessment

Gaining buy-in

A stress audit will provide evidence for the organisational leaders upon which to establish action plans for dealing with stress. Having a senior audit champion helps to give the audit impetus and momentum. The chief executive, human resources director or another director of the organisation as a champion will help to raise the profile of the audit and ensure that subsequent preventative work stays on the agenda at senior levels. Furthermore, an audit raises expectations among staff that preventative work will be undertaken. It is important to ensure that board commitment for post-audit action is established.

At Somerset CC the stress audit was championed by the county personnel officer who offered personal backing for the project. The council also established an audit working party made up of personnel representatives from each of the key service areas including education, social services and environment and planning. The group also included trade union officials whose involvement was a key element of the project.

Deciding on the survey instrument – ASSET

ASSET is a validated and standardised stress-auditing instrument. The measure has been developed by Cary Cooper for Robertson Cooper Ltd. ASSET incorporates modern workplace stressors into a stressor-strain model of stress, measuring the perceived threat of each stressor, and any strain outcomes in the form of psychological strain and stress-related physical ill-health (see Figure 7.2). It also measures lifestyle indicators such as one's exercise regime. It has been standardised and validated using a large sample of public and private sector organisations in the United Kingdom.

Deciding on the sample

Somerset CC is a large organisation with around 14,500 permanent members of staff. Although a stratified sampling approach could have been used, the working party felt that surveying the whole permanent staff population was the best approach to use. This way, the results could be easily generalisable to the whole population, and the sample sizes were sufficient to ensure that the results were representative of all of the demographic cells. Apart from the

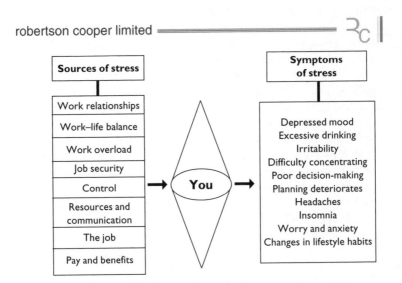

Figure 7.2 The Cooper model of stress.

statistical reasons for using the whole population, the working party wanted to ensure that everybody had the chance to participate. This was the largest survey of staff attitude that the council had ever undertaken and it was important to ensure that staff actually responded. It was felt that the adoption of a policy of inclusion would improve response rates.

Managing the project

The demographics are the basis of analysis; they determine how sensitive the statistical analysis can be in identifying hotspots within the organisation. Somerset CC used detailed demographics to ensure that all key work groups could be identified. This entailed actually printing four different surveys for each of the key departments within the council: education, social services, county hall based staff (including environment and planning and all of the support functions) and the fire brigade. Having four separate questionnaires meant the demographics could be tailored and made relevant for all staff.

Extensive corporate communications activities were initiated: written literature such as posters, fliers and staff reminders enclosed with staff payslips; a dedicated webpage on the council intranet including frequently asked questions and important telephone numbers such as those for the occupational health service and for human resources; and a dedicated helpline for those wishing to speak directly to someone about the audit.

One of the key issues in an audit of this nature is the issue of confidentiality. Staff need to feel confident that their responses are kept confidential. For this reason, RCL take steps to give them this confidence. ASSET is delivered to staff directly. Although ASSET can be delivered electronically over a secure website, in the case of Somerset CC, it was delivered in paper and pencil format to the home address of all staff. The covering letter assured them of the confidential nature of their responses. RCL also provided a pre-paid envelope so that staff could seal their completed surveys and send them directly back to RCL offices.

Results

The meticulous preparation and the corporate communication activities led to a high response rate. An average of 48 per cent of staff across each of the departments responded to the survey.

The key themes emerging from the results were as follows:

- Overall, the health of the sample was good. Health scores were better than those found in the UK general population norm set. There were few differences between departments with social services reporting marginally poorer psychological health compared to the norm set.
- Overall, the stressor profile indicated that 'Work Overload' was the main stressor factor followed closely by 'Job Security and Change'.
- Closer inspection of the two key stressor factors showed that there were specific aspects of these two stressor factors that were most problematic. The key 'Work Overload' item was 'I do not have enough time to do the job as well as I would like'. Having unmanageable workloads was not an issue; neither was having to work to unrealistic deadlines (see Figure 7.3). This can be interpreted as something of an indictment of modern working practices where a high volume of work can be delivered

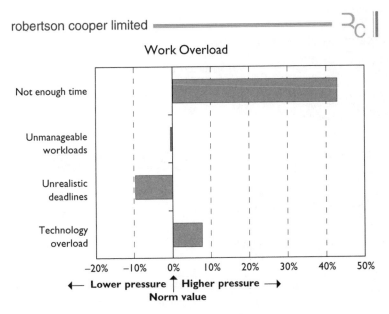

Figure 7.3 Item analysis of the 'Work Overload' factor.

© Robertson Cooper Ltd 2002. All rights reserved.

but people generally feel that there is a compromise on their own standards of work quality.

- The key item on the 'Job Security and Change' factor was 'My job is likely to change in the future'. Staff generally felt that job security was not a key stressor (see Figure 7.4). This is a reflection of the massive change that local authority staff have been experiencing since the early 1990s. Continual change can be stressful and can result in wear and tear on staff.

With such a large dataset, a whole range of results were generated including the following:

- The threat of physical violence was a key stressor for many staff, especially those working in social services and in education.
- Long hours of work was also rated as a key stressor for a majority of staff and long hours were prevalent most especially among teachers.
- Technological overload was a problem for the majority of staff (having to deal with new technology – particularly email).

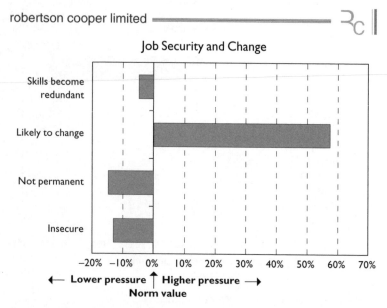

Figure 7.4 Item analysis of the 'Job Security and Change' factor.

- For senior social workers, work overload was particularly problematic as was having to deal with difficult clients.
- Main grade teachers reported poorer health than that found in the norm set.
- Only about half of staff had attended their annual appraisal.
- Work relationships across the whole sample were far better than those in the norm set.
- Employee commitment was also far better across the whole sample than that found in the norm set.

The council has been particularly careful to ensure that the audit process is as open and as objective as possible. Not only was there widespread coverage of the audit through corporately managed communications, but also the results of the audit have been openly communicated at both the departmental level and at the corporate level.

Stress interventions

Following an audit such as this it is necessary to design interventions that deal with the issues that the audit has raised. Knowing where the hotspots are and knowing why it is a hotspot helps to ensure that intervention can be planned efficiently and targeted in the right place. Somerset CC has followed the audit with a series of action plans. There is an action plan for each directorate with the lead director for each directorate acting as the individual responsible for delivering the action plan. At the corporate level, there is also an action plan with the county personnel officer taking responsibility for its delivery.

Table 7.1 shows a short extract from the Corporate Action Plan. It includes a brief description of an issue identified from the stress audit, the council response to the issue, those responsible for carrying out the response, how the response may be related to other activities already going on in the council, and the target date for delivery of the response.

There are specific elements of the action plan that deal with employees from identified hotspots. For example, training for employees in how to deal with pressure, and the purchase of multi-media solutions for use by employees for raising awareness of stress issues. A significant financial sum of money has been agreed by the executive and can be accessed by departments and corporately to put into place specific planned actions.

Table 7.1 Extract from the Somerset Corporate Action Plan

Problem identified	Response action	Responsibility	Links to other plans/existing processes	Date for completion
Nature of the work • Emotionally demanding • Potential for violence/ threats/verbal abuse	Line managers to identify jobs of this nature and improve the person specification to take account of key competencies and personal attributes Nature of work to be clarified during recruitment	All line managers	Departmental action plans	Ongoing
	Review recruitment and selection guidelines and content of supporting training	County personnel department		December 2002
	Enable more flexible deployment of staff through secondments, job rotation and job share	Line managers and county personnel department		March 2003
	Develop a corporate system for improved monitoring of threats of violence and verbal abuse and debriefing mechanism	County personnel department	Race Equality Scheme and Plan, Corporate Equality Plan	March 2003
Workload	Identify where there are particular needs for higher level project management or workflow planning skills amongst managers, and consider best way to develop these (e.g., consultancy support, senior manager mentoring/coaching, provision of training, etc.)	Line manager to identify needs and discuss with Training and Development		March 2003

	Action	Responsibility		Timescale
Email • Quantity • 'Flame' mail	Senior management to promote and encourage an effective work–life balance (e.g. avoiding breakfast and evening meetings)	Senior management team and cascade to other line managers		As soon as possible
	Develop guidance to employees on use of email	County personnel and IT	Info. Mgt. Policy being developed	December 2002
General fitness • Not identified as problem (health generally good), but exercise medically recognised as alleviating effects of stress	Work with Somerset Catering Services (SCS) to promote healthier eating amongst the workforce	SCS		December 2003
	Publicity campaign to employees about the value of physical exercise	Occupational health	European Health and Safety Week October 2002	Ongoing

Some of the actions did not require significant financial invest-ments. Elements of the action plan were more about reprioritising how resources and management effort were directed (for example, senior management role modelling of better work–life balance working practices by avoiding breakfast and evening meetings).

The Somerset CC post-audit action plans are now absorbed into the council performance management processes and their success will be evaluated mainly through the council EFQM (European Foundation for Quality Management) audits because these processes are already established at the council and take place on an annual basis. The council have set themselves performance targets that are directly related to the issues raised in the stress audit including:

- an increase in the percentage of staff who undergo formal appraisal;
- an increase in the percentage of staff who regularly exercise;
- increase in staff using flexible working arrangements;
- undertaking a council-wide recruitment audit;
- reductions in stress-related sickness absence;
- to re-audit with ASSET on a regular basis those parts of the organisation that were considered to be hotspots.

As well as compiling action plans at both the corporate level and at the departmental level, it is important in any stress management programme to emphasise the responsibilities that staff have for managing their own stress. Managers cannot and indeed should not have the responsibility for the whole vista of a person's life pressures. Non-work related stress, personal coping strategies and personal lifestyle choices are the personal responsibility of every individual in the organisation. Minimising stress levels through lifestyle changes and improved personal exercise regimes by staff need to run alongside organisational efforts to deal with underlying work related stressors. It is important to reinforce the message that stress management is a partnership between the organisation and its staff.

Somerset CC has undertaken to train all of its managers in understanding this relationship so that they can help themselves and their own team members to deal with personal stress. All of the managers across the council have undergone stress awareness training.

Summary

Auditing based on a measure of stress using validated sources and symptoms of stress provides an organisation with a method for applying the HSE's principle of prevention. It will highlight the stress hotspots in the organisation in terms of job role, level of seniority, age, gender and other relevant demographics, and provide evidence upon which to base targeted action planning.

The extent to which significant improvements in stress levels are achieved is entirely dependent upon the post auditing activity that is undertaken. A commitment to subsequent action planning will improve the quality of working lives of staff. Gaining commitment from managers to act on the results of the audit is the most beneficial way of dealing with concerns such as 'What if I don't like the audit results?', 'How much information should I share with my staff?' and 'What's the use, it won't make any difference?' In committing to post-audit action planning managers can say that no matter what the results are like, the concern is about making things better.

Stage one: assessment of job stress

The case study highlights best practice in conducting a stress audit within an organisation. Stage one of the risk management process involves preparation (gaining commitment from all parties, budgeting, planning and an assessment of the cost of stress); identification of hazards (measuring levels of perceived stressors in the workplace); assessment of the associated risks (measuring the levels of stress outcomes, such as psychological well-being). Initially, preparation involved gaining the commitment of all parties in the organisation; this was achieved through, identifying a senior audit champion (the chief executive, human resources director or another director of the organisation), and establishing an audit working party, comprising personnel representatives from each of the key service areas and trade union officials. Senior management support for the audit is essential, not only for encouraging the participation of staff, but also for ensuring that the implementation of the stress prevention programme is successful. Psychosocial hazards (stressors) were identified using a stress audit tool, in this case ASSET. It is important that the measuring instrument is based on an adequate theoretical framework, and has established reliability and validity. The audit was conducted across the organisation, but also focused on specific occupational groups, with an emphasis on identifying risk factors for those groups. For example, long hours of work was rated as a key stressor for a majority of staff, however, this stressor emerged as a particular problem for teachers. Finally, the audit identifies the risks associated with stressors, in terms of strain (in this case, psychological well-being and physical health were measured).

Summary

This chapter has examined a number of stress audit tools, including OSI, PMI and ASSET, which could be used to assess stress levels in an organisation. The case study illustrates the use of ASSET to identify stressors in the workplace for a UK county council. It outlines how a stress audit is conducted, including the identification of stress hotspots. This is the first stage of the risk management model. A discussion of how to conduct a risk assessment of psychosocial hazards (stressors) is developed in the following chapter, building on the data provided by the case study.

Chapter 8

Risk evaluation

At stage one of the risk management process, the objective is to identify hazards and to assess the level of harm being caused (either at an individual or organisational level). Employee-related outcomes that are frequently used as indicators of strain include measures of employees' physical health, psychological well-being and job satisfaction. Behavioural measures are less often included, but common measures are absenteeism and productivity. This chapter discusses the second stage of the risk management model, risk evaluation. This is an important stage, as it evaluates the extent of the harm caused by workplace stressors, that is the risk associated with the level of stress in the workplace. The situation for many organisations is that they are aware that occupational stress may pose a hazard, and that there are a number of effective ways that the associated harm can be mitigated, e.g. stress counselling. However, few conduct risk assessments that include an analysis to evaluate the extent to which hazards are likely to have negative outcomes. The calculation of *risk factors* allows some quantification of the risk associated with workplace stressors.

Risk factors

A risk factor is related to both the stress level (E) and the probability of a negative outcome (P). Risk control strategies need to consider both the stress level and the efficacy of individuals/groups at coping with the stress (the extent to which it is translated into negative outcomes). It is possible that a workplace demonstrates a high level of a particular stressor, such as *aspects of the job* (e.g. arduous physical working conditions); however, due to the levels of social support available within the work group and individuals' effective coping strategies, this stressor has little negative effect in terms of experienced psychological strain. In this case, the level of E could be quite high, but P is relatively low. Another workplace stressor, such as *work–life balance* (e.g. work demands spill over and interfere with individuals' home lives), could be rated as a moderate source of pressure, but due to the lack of organisational support for flexible working, there are considerable negative effects on employee well-being. In this case, the level of E is relatively low, but the level of P is high. Risk factors allow some prioritisation of remedial action. In the examples above, the introduction of more flexible working practices is likely to have a more positive effect on employee well-being than attempting to change fundamental aspects of the job itself, despite *work–life balance* being rated lower than *aspects of the job* as a source of pressure.

Calculation of risk factors

Data from the case study (described in Chapter 7) can be used to illustrate the calculation of risk factors associated with psychological strain. The measurement instrument ASSET was employed to conduct a stress audit, including the measurement of workplace stressors and outcome measures, including psychological well-being. The risk factors can be calculated using the following formula (as described in Chapter 6):

risk factor = exposure (E) × probability (P)

E – the perceived level of the stressor
P – likelihood of exposure to stressor resulting in negative outcome

Case study: assessing risk factors for employee well-being

Data from the stress audit instrument, ASSET, was used to obtain E (the level of perceived stress) for eight workplace stressors, and also psychological well-being, allowing the calculation of P (utilising the correlation between the level of a stressor and a stress outcome). In each case, the risk factor is the value of $E × P$.

Table 8.1 shows the mean perceived levels of stress associated with the eight sources of pressure and the correlations with psychological well-being (both measured using ASSET). Positive

Table 8.1 Sample risk factors for the ASSET stressors (N = 6,666)

Stressors	E*	r**	P***	Risk factor
Working relationships	2.27	0.41	17.06	39
Work–life balance	3.05	0.47	22.00	67
Overload	3.21	0.52	26.83	86
Job security	2.62	0.23	5.34	14
Control	3.05	0.38	14.06	43
Resources/communication	3.00	0.40	16.24	49
Your job	3.14	0.48	23.33	73
Pay and benefits	3.42	0.17	2.99	10

Notes:
* weighted means
** correlation between each stressor subscale and the psychological well-being subscale
*** $P = r^2 \times 100$.

correlations indicate that a stressor is associated with an increased level of negative psychological well-being. The final column indicates the 'risk factor' associated with each stressor.

The highest risk factors, for the sample of county council employees, are associated with *overload* (risk factor = 86), *aspects of your job* (risk factor = 73) and *work–life balance* (risk factor = 67). Employees are most at risk of developing symptoms of psychological strain as a result of overload, aspects of the job and work–life balance. Therefore, focusing efforts on these sources of pressure in the workplace will have the most positive effect on employee well-being. Other stressors have much lower risk factors, notably *pay and benefits*, which has a fairly high level of *E*, but is less likely (compared to other sources of stress) to have negative effects in terms of psychological well-being.

Interpreting risk factors

Risk factors take into account both the level of the stressor in the workplace (*E*) and the probability that negative stress outcomes will result (*P*). A range of stress outcomes could be employed, e.g. physical health, psychological well-being, job performance, sickness absence, work accidents. It is possible that different risk factors could be obtained for different outcomes, e.g. overload might have a high risk factor associated with physical health, but a lower risk factor associated with absenteeism. In this example, the effects of overload might be manifest as physical symptoms, e.g. headaches, insomnia or indigestion, rather than as absenteeism (perhaps due to an organisational culture characterised by presenteeism, the over-riding expectation that employees should attend work, even if they are feeling unwell). The inclusion of a range of outcome measures also allows for individual differences in terms of stress response, as there will be differences in the type of symptoms experienced by an individual in response to exposure to different stressors (Cooper *et al.* 1989). Thus, one individual may experience physical symptoms, while another experiences psychological symptoms.

As the measures used (means and correlations) aggregate across individuals, risk factors indicate the level of risk associated with particular stressors for the workforce, or work group, *as a whole*. While there may be stressors that pose a high level of risk across an organisation, it is likely that some stressors will be particularly salient for different occupations or work groups. In the case study, the threat of physical violence was a major stressor for staff working in social services and in education, and long hours of work was identified as most prevalent among teachers. Thus, it is important that risk factors are calculated for key work groups and depart-ments. The calculation of risk factors does not indicate particular individuals, or groups of individuals, who have a high risk of develop-ing stress symptoms. Individual differences, such as personality, can result in higher vulnerability for certain people. For example, individuals who display anger or hostility towards others (one dimension of Type A behaviour pattern) tend to be more prone to physical health problems (Ganster *et al.* 1991). Individual profiles should be examined to identify employees who seem to display particularly high levels of stress and/or difficulty in coping, or whose levels of health/well-being are very low. These individuals are 'high risk' and may benefit from individual-focused stress prevention measures, such as stress counselling or special work schedules. It is also possible that particular groups may have increased vulner-ability, e.g. parents of young children, older employees. A detailed analysis using demographic data can identify stressful conditions at this level.

Assessing safety risks

Although stress audits frequently include outcome measures such as employee health or psychological well-being, there is little emphasis on behavioural outcomes. Yet it is important that all the risks

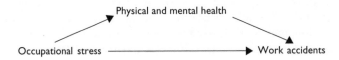

Figure 8.1 The relationship between job stress and work accidents.

associated with occupational stress are included in the audit, that is risks are considered not only in terms of ill-health, but also in relation to work accidents. Research evidence reviewed in this book (see Chapter 5) indicates that occupational stress is linked to work accidents directly and indirectly, mediated by the effects of occupational stress on employee health (see Figure 8.1). In order to incorporate stress audits within a broader risk management process, there is a need to include a range of outcomes, relevant to both health and safety outcomes.

The following case study illustrates the risk assessment of job stress and accidents in a sample of offshore oil workers (source: Valerie Sutherland, Sutherland-Bradley Associates).

Case study: managing stress and accidents in the offshore oil and gas industry

Introduction

This case study describes a stress audit used to understand occupational stress and accidents in the offshore oil and gas exploration and production industry; 310 males took part in this work environment risk assessment of drilling and production installations on the Continental Shelf in the North and Celtic seas.

The links between stress and accident involvement are established but less well documented than the recognised relationships between stress and ill-health. Nevertheless, it is acknowledged that a person under stress is 'an accident about to happen'. Therefore, of key interest in this unique and potentially dangerous and hazardous work environment was the impact of stress on accident occurrence and the psychological well being of the offshore worker.

Conducting a stress audit

The objectives of the audit were to

- identify the key sources of stress in the offshore environment;
- examine the links between accident involvement, job satisfaction, mental health and perceptions of stress offshore;
- measure differences in stress levels and accident rates in relation to occupational status (contractor versus permanent, operator personnel) and offshore environment (e.g. location, type and size of installation);
- investigate style of behaviour as a causal factor in accident involvement;
- examine the role of social support as a moderator of accidents.

Data generated from a series of one-to-one interviews were used to develop a stressor item bank unique to offshore workers. In addition to rating sources of stress, the workforce was also asked to provide information on

- accident involvement both onshore and offshore
- personal and career demographics
- exercise and relaxation behaviours
- alcohol and tobacco consumption
- change in work and personal circumstances
- personality and behavioural style
- social support at work and at home
- job satisfaction
- psychological health.

The questionnaire package was administered by post.

Results

Career demographics

Results indicated that the offshore worker was experienced and well qualified. Over 70 per cent had spent five years or more working offshore; half had experience of working on both drilling and production installations and almost three-quarters held technical qualifications. The most common work pattern involved working twelve-hour shifts (a mix of days and nights), for a period of fourteen days, followed by fourteen days off. Seven different nationalities working on ninety-seven installations were identified and took part in the audit. Ages ranged from 21 to 60, with 26 per cent of the sample between 31 and 35 years. Almost three-quarters were married, and 12 per cent were either divorced or separated.

Accidents offshore

Some 29 per cent of offshore personnel reported an accident leading to personal injury during their offshore career. Of the seventy-five personnel providing full details, 7 per cent indicated that they were injured during the first or second day of a tour of duty and 16 per cent were injured during the last two days. Thus, these findings did not support the official statistics that suggest most incidents occur at these times, that is, when personnel are settling in to a new work routine, or anticipating the return home.

Consistent with official statistics, a higher rate of accidents was reported by personnel working on drilling rigs (37 per cent) compared to production platform employees (23 per cent). No difference was observed in the number of accidents reported by operator staff (permanent contract) and the contract personnel.

Personnel involved in an accident leading to personal injury reported a poorer level of mental health than the accident-free respondents. Although the reported job satisfaction levels between the two groups did not significantly differ, the expected trend was observed. However, job satisfaction levels were already very low for this occupational group, independent of accident involvement, and so the measure may not have been sensitive enough to detect any further detriment. Personnel who had remained accident free were less likely to be cigarette smokers (29 per cent) than the accident victim group (43 per cent were smokers). The opportunity to smoke is extremely limited during the twelve-hour work shift and authorised smoking areas are very restrictive during leisure time. Therefore, the physiological effects of nicotine craving should be investigated. For example, an accident could occur if the individual was finding it hard to concentrate or function properly.

Stress and accidents

A trend for accident victims to report more stress than those who remained accident free was noted. Operator personnel who had been involved in an accident perceived higher levels of stress from

- The home–work interface (e.g. leaving one's family to cope;

problem unwinding on return home; family never seeing where I work);

- lack of career prospects and reward (e.g. lack of job security; lack of promotion opportunities; rate of pay);
- the physical climate and work (e.g. the severe weather conditions; unpleasant conditions due to cold; the hazardous or dangerous environment).

Contractor personnel who had been involved in an accident reported more stress associated with 'career prospects and reward' and the 'physical climate and work' than their accident-free counterparts.

Stressor predictors of accident involvement among the permanent (operator) staff included 'work overload' (i.e. pay cuts due to the recession; extra responsibility; working excessive periods of time offshore with only short breaks) and the stress associated with the home–work interface.

Although the initial stress audit did not permit us to make any assumptions about accident causation, the opportunity to repeat the audit process over an eighteen-month period offered the chance to investigate causality. Thus, measures taken to assess the impact of an accident indicated that offshore personnel became more anxious, and exhibited a poorer level psychological well-being following an incident. However, there was also a trend for this group to report poorer psychological health prior to the accident, but this was further reduced following the event. It is suggested that psychological state may be a causal factor in accidents, and being involved in an accident further exacerbates this condition. There was also a trend for those involved in an accident to perceive the work environment as more stressful. Compared to those who remained accident free, accident victims reported higher levels of stress related to

- the home–work interface;
- lack of career prospects and reward;
- safety and insecurity (e.g. not knowing how safe the installation is; helicopter travel; inadequate instruction to do the job, etc.);
- the physical climate and work.

Conclusion

A risk assessment of physical hazards in the work environment is a legal requirement. However, accidents are not caused by a single event, but by a chain of events. By identifying the psychosocial and psychological factor associated with accident vulnerability, the stress audit can improve the risk assessment process. It is a proactive way to identify stress hazards, who might be affected and how. The objective is to control stress, reduce accidents at work and optimise business profitability.

Stage two: risk evaluation

The case study highlights two particular sources of stress that predicted work accidents (for permanent operators): *work overload* (e.g. pay cuts due to the recession; extra responsibility; working excessive periods of time offshore with only short breaks) and the *home–work interface* (e.g. leaving one's family to cope; problem unwinding on return home; family never seeing where I work). In the case study above, the stress audit was based on a tailor-made survey of stressors specific to the work environment (for examples of offshore stressors, see Box 8.1).

The findings suggested that individuals with poorer psychological health were more likely to be accident involved, and that psychological health deteriorated further following an accident. These findings support the direct and indirect influence of occupational stress on accident involvement (proposed in previous chapters).

Box 8.1 Examples of stressors for workers on offshore oil platforms

1 Working in a hazardous/dangerous environment
2 I don't feel enough is done towards personal safety
3 The routine nature of the job
4 Sometimes I feel I don't have time to do the job properly
5 The variety and uncertainty in my job
6 Working long hours
7 Boredom – not enough to do
8 Working fourteen days on/off
9 Last minute changes in crew arrangements
10 Keeping up with changes in new equipment
11 Travel by helicopter
12 Working in severe weather conditions

Source: adapted from Sutherland and Cooper (1986).

Including outcome measures that relate to both employee health and safety allow the assessment of a broader range of risks. However, there are difficulties associated with assessing safety risks.

Problems associated with accident measures

The calculation of risk factors can be difficult where safety outcomes are measured in terms of accidents. Individual employees are unlikely to experience many accidents, leading to an outcome measure that provides skewed data, with very few individuals within the sample reporting accidents in comparison to those who report nil. In the previous case study, comparisons are made between individuals who have experienced an accident versus those who have not. Unless accidents are measured prospectively, there can be difficulties in interpreting the stress–accident relationship. There can also be problems associated with under-reporting, which is widely acknowledged as a significant issue across industries. The problem of under-reporting applies particularly to incidents not involving equipment failure or damage (Trommelen 1991), but extends to the failure to report quite serious occupational injuries (Powell *et al.* 1971; Senneck 1975). Mandatory reporting schemes have been reinforced through automatic logging systems, e.g. signals passed at danger by the railway industry, and legal requirements, e.g. the reporting of near-misses in aviation. However, the recording of many incidents still depends on the individual worker to complete the relevant paperwork.

Under-reporting and the suppression of information has been linked to the existence of a *blame culture*, where the purpose of collecting accident and incident data is to apportion blame and take disciplinary action (Adams and Hartwell 1977; Webb *et al.* 1989). A degree of trust is required for workers to report incidents. Some organisations have implemented confidential reporting schemes to this end (e.g. the US Aviation Safety Reporting System: see Reynard *et al.* 1986 for further details), while others have endeavoured to create a *no blame culture*, which encourages the reporting of incidents as a means of improving safety, rather than to apportion blame (Turner 1991; van der Schaaf 1991). Certain industries have a macho work environment, e.g. construction, which discourages reporting (Glendon 1991). Reporting can also be undermined where relatively minor incidents are regarded as routine and 'part of the day's work' (Clarke 1998a).

Review of alternative measures

Recognition of the difficulties involved in using actual accidents as an outcome measure has prompted researchers to develop alternative measures. Zohar (2002b) used minor reportable injuries recorded by the medical staff at the company infirmary. The injuries recorded over a six-month period formed a uniform, non-skewed distribution. Hemingway and Smith (1999) recorded near-injuries, in addition to reported and unreported injuries. The study found that all categories of injuries were significantly predicted by occupational stressors, although different stressors were associated with the different outcome measures. Hofmann and Stetzer (1996) developed a checklist of twenty-three unsafe behaviours, e.g. using a tool to prop open a door, climbing stairs two at a time, where respondents would rate the frequency of engaging in the behaviours. This scale had an alpha coefficient of 0.89.

In addition to recording negative outcomes, such as accidents, injuries and near-misses, positive safety behaviours have also been used as outcome measures. Cheyne *et al.* (1998) developed a measure of employees' *participation in safety activities*; it comprises a checklist of sixteen activities, where respondents indicate the frequency of their involvement (e.g. being involved in accident investigations, taking part in job safety analyses) (although no reliability data are presented). Geller *et al.* (1996) report a nine-item scale measuring the *propensity to actively care*, e.g. reminding co-workers of hazards, confronting others about unsafe acts, picking up after others to maintain good housekeeping, correcting potential safety hazards where possible. The reliability of the scale is reported as alpha coefficients of 0.79 and 0.83, for two different samples. Griffin and Neal (2000) identified two separate components of safety-related performance: safety compliance and safety participation. Two subscales, each comprising four items, were developed to measure compliance with safety procedures ($\alpha = 0.94$), e.g. 'I use the correct safety procedures for carrying out my job', and participation in safety-related activities ($\alpha = 0.89$), e.g. 'I voluntarily carry out tasks or activities that help to improve workplace safety' (Neal *et al.* 2000).

Glendon and Litherland (2001) developed a behavioural observation measure, which used behaviour sampling to observe samples of behaviour at random intervals to determine safe performance (e.g. wearing personal protective equipment, traffic awareness, housekeeping, using correct procedures). This method is a fairly involved and labour-intensive process, but provides objective measurement of employees' behaviour. However, the authors failed to find a relationship between safety performance and safety climate factors. They concluded that the behavioural measure was too focused on observable aspects, such as wearing hard hats, and did not reflect the full range of safety performance.

The calculation of risk factors depends on the use of valid and reliable measures. There are a number of options, in addition to records of actual accidents, including occupational injuries (Zohar 2002b), unsafe behaviours (Hofmann and Stetzer 1996) and questionnaire scales (Neal et al. 2000), which have proven validity and reliability. The use of such outcome measures would allow the calculation of the safety risks of occupational stress.

Risk control

The design of an intervention programme, including risk control measures, involves a number of processes, including an assessment of the *acceptability* of the risk factors identified, a review of existing initiatives and programmes within the company and an analysis of the costs involved in implementation.

Risk factors derived from the stress audit (stage one) refer specifically to the samples involved. These can be compared between work groups and departments to identify areas of high risk for particular stressors within the organisation. In order to judge the acceptability of risks, in terms of normative populations, e.g. is a risk factor significantly higher than that obtained for other similar organisations, the development of risk factor norms is needed. The decision as to the acceptability of a risk must then be determined by considering the level of the risk factor in relation to the norm, taking into account the cost of lowering the risk level against the benefits from a reduction in risk.

There is no simple translation from risk assessment to risk control measure, whereby a certain solution can always be prescribed for identified problems. Each intervention program should be tailor-made for the organisation involved, considering the existing initiatives and developments already operating within the company; a piecemeal approach, where specific solutions are targeted at single risk factors, should be avoided (Kompier 1996; Cox et al. 2000). Cox et al. (2000) recommend that the process of translation should involve the identification of *underlying pathologies*. For example, the analysis of stress audit data might have revealed high risk factors for *work relationships* (unsupportive relationships with superiors), *work–life balance* (difficulty maintaining a satisfactory balance between work responsibilities and personal/home life) and *control* (lack of influence in the way in which work is organised and performed). Further investigation of these factors, e.g. through consultation and discussion with representatives of the workforce, might suggest a connection between these factors, e.g. that an authoritarian management style is the root of the problem, resulting in unsupportive working relationships, inflexible management attitudes towards work schedules and over-managing. Therefore, risk control measures aimed at changing management style, rather than three separate measures targeted at each source of stress, would be advisable, possibly incorporated into existing stress reduction programmes aimed at managers.

Summary

This chapter has discussed the process of risk evaluation, based on the calculation of risk factors. Interpreting risk factors helps to identify areas of concern, where there is a significant probability that the current level of a stressor is resulting in negative outcomes for the workforce. The case study, examining stress and accidents for offshore oil workers, illustrates the causal relationship between stress and work accidents, and the utility of including safety risks within hazard assessments. The possibility of including safety outcomes is discussed, including a review of valid and reliable measures of safety-related behaviours. Risk control measures need to be implemented to reduce unacceptable risks; however, the design of intervention programmes cannot be prescriptive. The final stage, risk reduction, is discussed in Chapter 9.

Chapter 9

Risk reduction

This chapter discusses how organisations can use the information gained from the stress audit and risk evaluation stages of the risk management approach, including an overview of past stress interventions. The final stage involves the implementation and monitoring of stress prevention and reduction measures. There is substantial evidence to suggest that many stress reduction programmes, such as employee assistance programmes (EAPs), are very effective in mitigating the symptoms of stress (Cooper and Sadri 1991; Berridge *et al.* 1997; Highley-Marchington and Cooper 1998). However, much of the evidence is focused on tertiary measures, which are aimed at individuals who display stress-related symptoms, such as stress counselling. Cox *et al.* (2000) recommend that an intervention package could include tertiary action, but that measures should also be implemented at primary and secondary levels (i.e., should involve preventative action). A description of the levels of stress intervention is presented in Box 9.1.

However, reviews of stress intervention programmes (Burke 1993; Cooper and Payne 1988; Cox 1993; International Labour Organisation 1992; Kahn and Byosiere 1992; Karasek 1992) suggest that such programmes frequently fail to emphasise prevention at the source.

Due to the structure of health care costs, there has been a strong financial incentive for US employers to introduce stress prevention programmes. The focus of the programmes is the prevention of individual ill-health, thus they tend to emphasise the health-related behaviour of workers in relation to specific health problems. There is little impetus for US companies to introduce programmes that include worker participation or changes to the work environment. There are differences in Europe, where preventative action is more

---

Box 9.1 A description of stress management interventions

Primary level

Scope: preventative – reduce number and/or
            intensity of stressors
Target: alter work environments, technologies or
            organisational structures
Examples: job redesign, employee participation, flexible
            working

Secondary level

Scope: preventative/reactive – modify individuals'
            responses to stressors
Target: individual
Examples: stress management training, communication and
            information sharing

Tertiary level

Scope: treatment – minimise damaging consequences of
            stressors by helping individuals cope more
            effectively
Target: individual
Examples: employee assistance programmes, stress
            counselling

Source: adapted from Cooper *et al.* (2001).

---

common. In the United Kingdom, for example, programmes tend to focus on stress management (e.g. training, health promotion programmes and employee counselling services), while in Scandinavia, there is a greater emphasis on job redesign and organisational change. In a review of European stress intervention programmes, Geurts and Grundemann (1999) concluded that

- preventative and work environment focused activities tended to be directed at the reduction of physical rather than psychosocial stressors;
- the type of programme was predicted by motivations such as 'staff morale' and 'legislation';

- most stress prevention programmes were initiated by management, rather than trade unions, particularly in large organisations.

Much of the work in conducting cost-benefit analyses on stress
interventions has been undertaken in the United States (Mossink
and Licher 1998), with a limited amount in Europe (Cooper *et al.*
1996). A review of stress intervention practice (Cooper *et al.* 1996),
presented to the European Commission, reports examples of
significant cost benefits over and above implementation costs.
However, much of the evidence is focused on employee health
outcomes (e.g. sickness absence), with little evidence related to
accident reduction.

Secondary/tertiary stress prevention

Part of the function of the risk management model is to identify
'high risk' individuals and groups of individuals. These employees
may show an indication of being 'under stress', such as high
perceived stress levels and ineffective coping strategies, or report
high levels of physical or psychological ill-health as a reaction to
stressors. In the former case, secondary action is needed to prevent
employees from developing stress-related symptoms, e.g. through
increasing their capacity to cope with stressors. In the latter case,
employees are already suffering stress-related illness and require
treatment activities (tertiary action), e.g. stress counselling,
rehabilitation and psychotherapy.

   The secondary and tertiary levels of intervention often focus on
the individual, either through programmes that encourage more
healthy lifestyles, e.g. keep-fit centres on site, dietary advice,
relaxation and exercise classes, or provide education on how to
develop more effective stress management skills. Tertiary interventions act to mitigate the symptoms of stress on an individual, e.g.
helping individuals to cope with their anxiety through relaxation
and biofeedback. The positive effects of an improved lifestyle can
feed back into the stress process by boosting individuals' resistance
to stress. Counselling is effective in improving the psychological
well-being of employees by increasing their confidence and self-
esteem (Berridge *et al.* 1997). Secondary interventions operate by
improving the coping strategies of individuals and/or by replacing

maladaptive coping styles with more successful ones, such as making employees less vulnerable to stress. Based on self-report measures, stress management activities would seem to have a modest effect in temporarily reducing experienced stress (Cooper *et al.* 1996; Murphy 1988), although the positive effects tend to diminish in the long term.

Although secondary and tertiary levels of stress intervention are effective when targeted at 'high risk' individuals or groups, there has been a tendency for organisations to employ such programmes for the workforce as a whole. This has been described as the *inoculation approach* to stress, as it focuses on the consequences, rather than the sources of stress, reflecting the attitude that stress is an inherent and enduring feature of the working environment. Such stress interventions will lower the risk factor associated with workplace stressors, by reducing the value of P (a more stress resistant workforce will have a reduced likelihood of experiencing stress symptoms), rather than by affecting the value of E, exposure to stressors. This approach can be very successful, particularly in the short term. US figures have demonstrated that companies made savings to investment rates of between 3:1 and 15:1 following the introduction of stress counselling (Cooper and Cartwright 1994). Cooper and Sadri (1991) found that an in-house stress counselling programme in a large organisation reduced absenteeism by 60 per cent in one year. However, isolated programmes can have temporary effects in the reduction of experienced stress (Murphy 1988). Although stress symptoms are reduced as a result of treatment and job perceptions become more positive, these changes decay over time as employees return to an unchanged work environment, with the same level of exposure to stressors. There is also the danger that such programmes tend to attract the 'worried well' (Sutherland and Cooper 1990), rather than those who most need help, particularly where the programmes are used across the workforce, rather than being targeted at individuals who are 'high risk'. While companies have tended to focus stress management activities at the managerial level, there is evidence to suggest that blue-collar workers, who tend to come from lower socio-economic groups, are more prone to heavy smoking, alcohol abuse, obesity and coronary heart disease. Thus, workers as well as managers can benefit from stress management programmes, particularly those aimed at lifestyle changes.

Primary stress prevention

Primary level interventions focus on stressor reduction. For example, where the nature of the job is leading to stress, the task or the work environment might be subject to redesign; where the organisation's structure or climate is the source of stress, a more participative management style might be encouraged (see Table 9.1). These interventions reduce exposure to stressors, lowering the value of E, and therefore reducing the risk factor. Such measures are most often considered in relation to changing the work environment (e.g. job enrichment, worker participation, career development activities,

Table 9.1 Primary level stress prevention strategies

Stressor	Possible strategies	
Work relationships	Opportunities for social interaction	Establish fair employment policies, build cohesive teams
Work–life balance	Flexitime, compressed work week, job sharing, stable and predictable rotating shifts	Establish flexible work schedules
Overload	Allow for recovery from demanding tasks, increased control over work pace	Analyse work roles and establish goals
Job security	Clear information on opportunities for promotion and career development	Include the employee in career development
Control		Encourage participative management
Resources and communication		Provide social support and feedback
Pay and benefits		Share the rewards
Aspects of the job	Job rotation, enrichment, opportunity to use skills, provide meaning and stimulation	Redesign the task, redesign the work environment
Cartwright and Cooper (2002)	NIOSH (1986)	Elkin and Rosch (1990)

team building, social support, etc.), but may also be targeted at individuals or groups (e.g. selection, pre-employment medical examination, health promotion and wellness programmes) (Kompier 1996). Cox *et al.* (2000) consider training to be primary prevention, rather than secondary, as it enhances task-related knowledge and skills.

There is a relatively limited amount of literature on risk reduction at the primary level, as few studies have focused on job redesign (Israel *et al.* 1996). However, a few studies have reported positive effects in terms of productivity and absenteeism. Brulin and Nilsson (1994) reviewed the findings of 1,500 projects funded by the Swedish Working Life Fund and found that productivity improved on average by 10 per cent, including production errors and delivery times. Terra (1995) reported a 50 per cent decrease in sickness absence following the introduction of job redesign and self-regulating teams.

Some aspects of the work environment may not be amenable to change, particularly certain aspects of the job itself, the level of job security or job-related pay and benefits. Stress intervention may be targeted at an individual level, e.g. through selection and recruitment procedures, to ensure that appropriate individuals are attracted and selected for these posts and that appropriate support and training is offered to help post-holders. (This is illustrated in the case study in Chapter 7, where the stress interventions include selection and recruitment, and training to deal with problems related to the nature of the work.)

Many jobs are characterised by high demands. One means of dealing with high demands can be to reduce them, but this may not always be practicable or desirable. The Karasek (1979) model defines high demand, low control jobs as stressful, but high control can mitigate the negative effects of high demands, creating a challenging 'active' job. Thus, increasing employee control can be used as a technique for reducing stress exposure. Control can be introduced in a number of ways, e.g. the use of autonomous work groups. Studies of such work groups have found positive effects on productivity and other work criteria, but a lack of improvement in well-being, motivation and absenteeism (e.g. Goodman *et al.* 1988). However, although many individuals will find that low control is a source of stress, there are individual differences in the degree of psychological strain experienced. For example, Fletcher and Jones

(1993) failed to replicate the interaction effect of high job demands and low job control on measures of strain predicted by Karasek's demand-control model. This is supported by research cited by de Rijk *et al.* (1998), who report a negative relationship between job autonomy and both emotional exhaustion and health complaints, only for those individuals with a high need for autonomy. The increased responsibility and decision latitude associated with greater autonomy can be perceived as an unwanted burden by some individuals, indicating that risk control measures centred around increasing employee autonomy will not be suitable for all employees. Employee participation and careful monitoring of the effects of any changes is needed when implementing risk control measures. Sparks *et al.* (2001) recommend that relevant training support is provided, e.g. where appropriate, problem-solving sessions could be held between supervisors and employees to identify job demands or stressors. Strategies could follow which increase the employees' perceived control so that they can cope more effectively (Spector 2000). Although stress interventions should be sensitive to individual differences, they should not be targeted at the individual, in terms of changing personality. For example, individuals who have high Type A behaviour pattern have greater susceptibility to stress, however, interventions might focus on skills training, to enable individuals to influence their own levels of stress through a reduction in interpersonal conflict (Jex 1998).

A detailed analysis of the risk assessment and evaluation stages of the risk management model can help to determine exactly what type of risk control measures are required, depending on the type of stressor. Moderate risks might be lowered by providing training or organisational support (reducing P), while a high risk might need an intervention at the organisational level (reducing E). If E is very high, reducing the value of P may be insufficient to reduce the overall value of the risk factor to an acceptable level, thus, organisational interventions must be aimed at reducing exposure. While some solutions can be relatively inexpensive, e.g. providing protective screens to protect bus drivers from the threat of physical violence, those aimed at changing the organisation's culture or structure can involve considerable expense. Using a risk management strategy allows companies to evaluate the relative level of risk involved, to justify expensive organisational development programmes.

Reducing safety risks

The majority of stress interventions are instigated with the intention to improve employee health outcomes, and therefore, positively influence outcomes of commercial relevance to organisations, such as absenteeism, productivity and compensation costs. However, such interventions are often fairly narrowly defined and conceptualised as health initiatives. Morrow and Crum (1998) note that interventions such as bonus pay, sensitivity training for supervisors, or provision of an on-site exercise facility tend to affect single outcomes, such as satisfaction with pay, supervision or stress, respectively; interventions which focus on safety improvements, particularly those which aim to change the safety culture, are 'not only the "right thing to do" but are one of the few managerial interventions that appear to have widespread effect'. The assessment of safety risks, in addition to health risks, within the risk management process, can allow the design of intervention programmes that influence both sets of outcomes. For example, health-promotion schemes can be employed to improve both health and safety outcomes. The positive benefits of health promotion programmes (e.g. improved diet, increased exercise, weight loss, smoking cessation, and the acquisition of stress-reduction techniques) have been demonstrated for employees' health (e.g. Demmer 1995; Dugdill and Springett 1994). Such programmes have also had favourable results for organisations, e.g. reductions in medical and disability costs, absenteeism and turnover, and enhanced corporate image (e.g. Conrad 1988; Daley and Parfitt 1996; Neck and Cooper 2000). However, there is little recognition that such programmes can be integrated into interventions aimed at safety risks. Mearns *et al.* (2003) found that fewer lost time injuries were significantly related to health promotion. The provision of health promotion programmes may influence safety outcomes in two ways; first, by demonstrating the company's concern for employee well-being, thus improving the safety climate, and second, improved worker health will provide increased resistance to stress and, therefore, reduced accident liability.

Morrow and Crum (1998) demonstrated that safety culture was strongly associated with a range of work-related attitudes, such as organisational commitment and job satisfaction. Neal *et al.* (2000) illustrated the links between organisational climate and the safety climate, suggesting that employees' evaluations of safety climate are made within the context of the general organisational climate. This finding suggests that interventions designed to improve the organisational climate can have a positive impact on safety climate. Thus, stress interventions aimed at changing corporate culture are likely to influence the safety climate.

In addition, safety interventions that are specifically targeted at improving the safety climate will be more effective when they are carried out within the context of a positive organisational climate. Interventions aimed at altering safety behaviour, e.g. reducing violations, can be targeted at changing the safety culture (Parker *et al.* 1995). Such an intervention would target the climate within which violations occur, rather than the behaviour itself (e.g. the strict enforcement of all rules and regulations). A safety climate which encourages an over-rigid application of rules and regulations creates a frame of reference within which behavioural consensus (compliance) is perceived as valued above appropriate (safe) conduct (Hopfl 1994); rather, the development of a 'just culture', that is 'an atmosphere of trust in which people are encouraged, even rewarded, for providing essential safety-related information, but in which they are also clear about where the line must be drawn between acceptable and unacceptable behaviour' (Reason 1997: 195). This line can be reinforced by rewarding acceptable behaviour and sanctioning unacceptable behaviour (as opposed to a 'no-blame' approach, where blame is not attached to actions). A safety-based intervention of this kind would be most effective as part of a broader intervention package aimed at improving employee communication throughout the organisation. Neal *et al.* (2000) suggest that interventions aimed solely at improving safety motivation (e.g. bonus and incentive schemes) are unlikely to be as effective as interventions that target both knowledge and motivation.

The synergy between organisational climate and safety climate suggests that interventions will be most effective, and will have the most wide-ranging effects, when they are the result of a systematic risk management process. It is suggested that the risk management model proposed in this book is applied to both the health *and* safety risks of occupational stressors. Thus, stress interventions are designed to reduce risks and have positive benefits for organisations in terms of employee health, health-related outcomes (e.g. sickness absence) and safety-related outcomes (e.g. lost time injuries, work accidents).

Stage three: risk reduction

The final stage of the risk management model involves monitoring the effects of risk control measures, and evaluating their effectiveness. The stress audit could be redistributed to identify the effects of the risk control measures in terms of levels of exposure and the effects of stressors on employee health. Indicators of organisational health, such as absenteeism, productivity, lost-time injuries and accident rates, should be monitored. Interventions aimed at safety risks, in addition to health risks, should evaluate the extent to which risk control measures have affected safety-related behaviour. Neal *et al.* (2000) recommend that incorporating assessments of knowledge, motivation, compliance, and participation into safety monitoring systems will provide a more complete assessment, not only of the effectiveness of safety practices, but also of their operation.

Employee participation is as important in this part of the process, as it is during the earlier stages. Interviews and focus groups with employees can help to identify the impact of measures on employees, assess their reactions and evaluate the extent to which the measures are having the desired effect. Any intervention programme needs to be ongoing, with the monitoring and review of the programme providing feedback to this process. Information from ongoing reviews can be used to adapt the programme to reflect changes in the organisation. The continuing nature of the programme will allow employees to take advantage of support as they need it. The provision of stress counselling can be useful, as many individuals may need this service at some point in their careers. Training can increase stress awareness, thus allowing individuals to recognise the symptoms of being 'under stress' and gives them to the knowledge of how to deal with stressors and recognise the point at which they would benefit from help and support.

Summary

This chapter has reviewed existing evidence of the effectiveness of stress interventions. While there is substantial evidence to support the effectiveness of secondary and tertiary interventions to help individuals manage job stress, there is limited evidence related to primary level interventions, due to their relative rarity. However, preventative action is most likely to be effective, particularly in the long term. An integrated package of intervention measures, tailor-made for the organisation, should include risk control measures that counteract both health and safety risks. The organisational climate affects both the safety climate and perceptions of occupational stress, thus broad level approaches are likely to have the most extensive effects on organisational health. There remains much work to be accomplished in the assessment and evaluation of safety risks. Further research is needed, particularly in relation to developing our understanding of the impact of psychosocial hazards on safety-related outcomes, such as accidents.

References

Adams, N.L. and Hartwell, N.M. (1977). Accident-reporting systems: A basic problem area in industrial society. *Journal of Occupational Psychology*, 50, 285–98.

Adelstein, A.M. (1952). Accident proneness: a criticism of the concept based upon an analysis of shunters' accidents. *Journal of the Royal Statistical Society*, 113, 354–400.

Alexander, M., Cox, S. and Cheyne, A. (1994). Safety culture within a UK based organisation engaged in offshore hydrocarbon processing. In *Proceedings of the Fourth Conference on Safety and Well-being at Work*. Loughborough: Centre for Hazard and Risk Management.

Aronsson, G., Gustafsson, K. and Dallner, M. (2000). Sick but yet at work: an empirical study of sickness presenteeism. *Journal of Epidemiology and Community Health*, 54, 502–9.

Arthur, W. and Graziano, W.G. (1996). The five-factor model, conscientiousness, and driving accident involvement. *Journal of Personality*, 64, 593–618.

Arthur, B., Barrett, G.V. and Alexander, R.A. (1991). Prediction of vehicular involvement: a meta-analysis. *Human Performance*, 4, 89–105.

Arthur, W., Strong, M.H. and Williamson, J. (1994). Validation of a visual attention test as a predictor of driving accident involvement. *Journal of Occupational and Organisational Psychology*, 67, 173–82.

Asfahl, R. (1984). *Industrial Safety and Health Management*. Englewood Cliffs, NJ: Prentice Hall.

Avolio, B.J., Kroeck, K.G. and Panek, P.E. (1985). Individual differences in information processing ability as a predictor of motor vehicle accidents. *Human Factors*, 27, 577–87.

Ballard, G.M. (1992). Industrial safety: safety by design. In J. Ansell and F. Wharton (eds) *Risk: Analysis, Assessment and Management*. Chichester: John Wiley.

Barling, J., Loughlin, C. and Kelloway, K. (2000). Development and test of a model linking transformational leadership and occupational safety.

Paper presented at the annual conference of the Society for Industrial and Organizational Psychology, New Orleans, LA.

Barling, J., Loughlin, C. and Kelloway, E.K. (2002). Development and test of a model linking safety-specific transformational leadership and occupational safety. *Journal of Applied Psychology*, 87, 488–96.

Barling, J., Kelloway, E.K. and Iverson, R.D. (2003). Accidental outcomes: attitudinal consequences of workplace injuries. *Journal of Occupational Health Psychology*, 8, 74–85.

Barrick, M.R. and Mount, M.K. (1991). The big five personality dimensions and job performance: a meta-analysis. *Personnel Psychology*, 44, 1–26.

Bass, B.M. (1985). *Leadership and Performance beyond Expectations*. New York: Free Press.

Bass, B.M. (1990). *Bass and Stogdill's Handbook of Leadership*. New York: Free Press.

Bate, P. (1984). The impact of organizational culture on approaches to organizational problem solving. *Organization Studies*, 5, 43–66.

Beard, K.M. and Edwards, J.R. (1995). Employees at risk: contingent work and the psychological experience of contingent workers. In C.L. Cooper and D.M. Rousseau (eds) *Trends in Organizational Behaviour*, vol. 2. Chichester: John Wiley.

Beehr, T. (1998). An organisational psychology meta-model of occupational stress. In C. Cooper (ed.) *Theories of Organisational Stress*. New York: Oxford University Press.

Beirness, D.J. (1993). Do we really drive as we live? The role of personality factors in road crashes. *Alcohol, Drugs and Driving*, 6, 129–43.

Benavides, F.G., Benach, J., Diez-Roux, A.V. and Roman, C. (2000). How do types of employment relate to health indicators? Findings from the Second European Survey on working conditions. *Journal of Epidemiology and Community Health*, 54, 494–501.

Berridge, J., Cooper, C.L. and Highley-Marchington, C. (1997). *Employee Assistance Programmes and Workplace Counselling*. Chichester: John Wiley.

Biesheuvel, S. and White, M.E. (1949). The human factor in flying accidents. *South African Air Force Journal*, 1, 25–36.

Blau, P.M. (1960). The theory of social integration. *American Journal of Sociology*, 65, 545–56.

Bolger, N. and Zuckerman, A. (1995). A framework for studying personality in the stress process. *Journal of Personality and Social Psychology*, 69, 890–902.

Borg, V., Kristensen, T.S. and Burr, H. (2000). Work environment and changes in self-rated health: a five year follow-up study. *Stress Medicine*, 16, 37–47.

Bortner, R. (1969). A short rating scale as a potential measure of Pattern A behaviour. *Journal of Chronic Diseases*, 22, 87–91.

Bosch, G. (1999). Working time: tendencies and emerging issues. *International Labour Review*, 138, 131–50.

Boyle, A.J. (1980). 'Found experiments' in accident research: report of a study of accident rates and implications for further research. *Journal of Occupational Psychology*, 53, 53–64.

Brewster, C., Mayne, L., Tregaskis, O., Parsons, D. and Atterbury, S. (1996). *Working Time and Contract Flexibility in Europe*. Cranfield, UK: Cranfield School of Management.

Brief, A.P. and George, J.M. (1991). Psychological stress and the workplace: a brief comment on Lazarus' outlook. *Journal of Social Behaviour and Personality*, 6, 15–20.

British Household Panel Survey (1998). In BBC news release, BBC 1's Panorama reveals nation of willing workaholics. BBC News Media Relations, 28 September.

Broadbent, D.E. (1987). *Perception and Communication*. London: Oxford University Press.

Broadbent, D.E., Cooper, P.F., Fitzgerald, P. and Parkes, K.R. (1982). The Cognitive Failures Questionnaire (CFQ) and its correlates. *British Journal of Clinical Psychology*, 21, 1–16.

Broadbent, D.E., Broadbent, M.H.P. and Jones, J.L. (1986). Performance correlates of self-reported cognitive failure and of obsessionality. *British Journal of Clinical Psychology*, 25, 285–99.

Brockner, J. (1988). *Self-esteem at Work: Research, Theory and Practice*. Lexington, MA: Lexington Books.

Brown, I.D. (1990). Drivers' margins of safety considered as a focus for research on error. *Ergonomics*, 33, 1307–14.

Brown, R.L. and Holmes, H. (1986). The use of a factor-analytic procedure for assessing the validity of an employee safety climate model. *Accident Analysis and Prevention*, 18, 445–70.

Brulin, G. and Nilsson, T. (1994). *Arbetsutveckling och forbattract producktvitet* (Development of work and improved productivity). Stockholm: Arbetslivfonden.

Buck, L. (1963). Errors in the perception of railway signals. *Ergonomics*, 6, 181–92.

Burke, M.J., Sarpy, S.A., Tesluk, P.E. and Smith-Crowe, K. (2002). General safety performance: a test of a grounded theoretical model. *Personnel Psychology*, 55, 429–57.

Burke, R.J. (1988). Sources of managerial and professional stress in large organizations. In C.L. Cooper and R. Payne (eds) *Causes, Coping and Consequences of Stress at Work*. New York: John Wiley.

Burke, R.J. (1993). Organisational level interventions to reduce occupational stressors. *Work and Stress*, 7, 77–87.

CARNET (The Canadian Aging Research Network) (1995). Flexible work arrangements: a user's guide. Guelph, Ontario: Psychology Department, University of Guelph.

Cartwright, S. and Cooper, C.L. (1997). *Managing Workplace Stress*. London: Sage.

Cartwright, S. and Cooper, C.L. (2002). *ASSET: Management Guide*. Manchester: Robertson Cooper Ltd.

Cartwright, S., Cooper, C.L. and Barron, A. (1996). The company car driver: occupational stress as a predictor of motor vehicle accident involvement. *Human Relations*, 49, 195–208.

Cass, M.H. (2003). A meta-analysis of the relationship between employee health and job satisfaction, job insecurity, management style and working hours. Unpublished PhD thesis, UMIST, Manchester.

Cassar, V. and Tattersall, A. (1998). Occupational stress and negative affectivity in Maltese nurses: testing moderating influences. *Work and Stress*, 12, 85–94.

Cellar, D.F., Nelson, Z.C., York, C.M. and Bauer, C. (2001). The five-factor model and safety in the workplace: investigating the relationships between personality and accident involvement. *Journal of Prevention and Intervention in the Community*, 22, 43–52.

Cheyne, A., Cox, S., Oliver, A. and Tomas, J.M. (1998). Modelling safety climate in the prediction of levels of safety activity. *Work and Stress*, 12, 255–71.

Clarke, S. (1994). Violations at work: implications for risk management. *Proceedings of the Fourth Conference on Safety and Well-being at Work*. Loughborough: Centre for Hazard and Risk Management.

Clarke, S. (1998a). Organizational factors affecting the incident reporting of train drivers. *Work and Stress*, 12, 6–16.

Clarke, S. (1998b). Safety culture on the UK railway network. *Work and Stress*, 12, 285–92.

Clarke, S. (1999). Perceptions of organizational safety: implications for the development of safety culture. *Journal of Organizational Behaviour*, 20, 185–98.

Clarke, S. (2000). Safety culture: under-specified and overrated? *International Journal of Management Reviews*, 2, 65–90.

Clarke, S. (2003). The contemporary workforce: its implications for organizational safety culture. *Personnel Review*, 32, 40–57.

Clement, R. and Jonah, B.A. (1984). Field dependency, sensation seeking and driving behavior. *Personality and Individual Differences*, 5, 87–93.

Cohen, A. (1977). Factors in successful occupational safety programs. *Journal of Safety Research*, 9, 168–78.

Cohen, A., Smith, M. and Cohen, H.H. (1975). *Safety Programs Practices in High vs. Low Accident Rate Companies – an Interim Report*. US Department of Health, Education and Welfare Publication 75-185. Cincinnati, OH: National Institute for Occupational Safety and Health.

Cohen, S. and Edwards, J. (1989). Personality characteristics as moderators of the relationship between stress and disorder. In W. Neufeld (ed.) *Advances in the Investigation of Psychological Stress.* New York: John Wiley.

Confederation of British Industry (CBI) (2000). *Focus on Absence.* London: CBI.

Conger, J.J., Gaskill, H.S., Glad, D.D., Rainey, R.V., Sawrey, W.L. and Turrell, E.S. (1957). Personal and interpersonal factors in motor vehicle accidents. *American Journal of Psychiatry*, 113, 1069–74.

Conger, J.J., Gaskill, H.S., Glad, D.D., Hassell, L., Rainey, R.V. and Sawrey, W.L. (1959). Psychological and psychophysical factors in motor vehicle accidents. *Journal of the American Medical Association*, 169, 1581–7.

Conrad, P. (1988). Worksite health promotion: the social context. *Social Science Medicine*, 26, 485–9.

Cooper, C.L. (1996). *The Handbook of Stress, Medicine and Health.* Boca Raton, FL: CRC Press.

Cooper, C.L. (1999). The changing psychological contract at work. *European Business Journal*, 11, 115–18.

Cooper, C.L. and Bramwell, R.S. (1992). A comparative analysis of occupational stress in managerial and shopfloor workers in the brewing industry: mental health, job satisfaction and sickness. *Work and Stress*, 2, 127–38.

Cooper, C.L. and Cartwright, S. (1994). Healthy mind; healthy organization – a proactive approach to occupational stress. *Human Relations*, 47, 455–71.

Cooper, C.L. and Marshall, J. (1976). Occupational sources of stress: a review of the literature relating to coronary heart disease and mental ill-health. *Journal of Occupational Psychology*, 49, 11–28.

Cooper, C.L. and Payne, R. (1988). *Causes, Coping and Consequences of Stress at Work.* New York: John Wiley.

Cooper, C.L. and Sadri, G. (1991). The impact of stress couselling at work. *Journal of Social Behaviour and Personality*, 6, 411–23.

Cooper, C.L. and Watson, M. (1991). *Cancer and Stress: Psychological, Biological and Coping Studies.* Chichester: John Wiley.

Cooper, C.L., Sloan, S.J. and Williams, S. (1988). *Occupational Stress Indicator Management Guide.* Windsor: NFER-Nelson.

Cooper, C.L., Rout, U. and Faragher, E.B. (1989). Mental health, job satisfaction and job stress among general practitioners. *British Medical Journal*, 298, 366–70.

Cooper, C.L., Liukkonen, P. and Cartwright, S. (1996). *Stress Prevention in the Workplace: Assessing the Costs and Benefits to Organisations.* European Foundation for the Improvement of Living and Working Conditions. Luxembourg: Office for Official Publications of the European Communities.

Cooper, C.L., Clarke, S. and Rowbottom, A. (1999). Occupational stress, job satisfaction and well-being in anaesthetists. *Stress Medicine*, 15, 115–26.

Cooper, C.L., Dewe, P.J. and O'Driscoll, M. (2001). *Organizational Stress: A Review and Critique of Theory, Research and Applications.* Thousand Oaks, CA: Sage.

Cooper, M.D. and Phillips, R.A. (1994). Validation of a safety climate measure. Paper presented at the BPS Occupational Psychology Conference, Birmingham, UK, January.

Cooper, M.D. and Phillips, R.A. (1995). Killing two birds with one stone: achieving quality via total safety management. *Leadership and Organization Development Journal*, 16, 3–9.

Costa, P.T. and McCrae, R.R. (1985). *The NEO Personality Inventory Manual.* Odessa, FL: Psychological Assessment Resources.

Cox, S. (1994). The promotion of safe working practices: a systems approach. Paper presented at the Safety and Well-Being at Work Conference, Loughborough, UK, November.

Cox, S. and Cox, T. (1991). The structure of employee attitudes to safety: a European example. *Work and Stress*, 5, 93–106.

Cox, S. and Cox, T. (1996). *Safety, Systems and People.* Oxford: Butterworth-Heinemann.

Cox, S. and Flin, R. (1998). Safety culture: philosopher's stone or man of straw? *Work and Stress*, 12, 189–201.

Cox, S., Tomas, J.M., Cheyne, A. and Oliver, A. (1998). Safety culture: the prediction of commitment to safety in the manufacturing industry. *British Journal of Management*, 9, 3–7.

Cox, T. (1978). *Stress.* London: Macmillan.

Cox, T. (1993). *Stress Research and Stress Management: Putting Theory to Work.* HSE Contract Report no. 61. Sudbury: HSE Books.

Cox, T. and Cox, S. (1993). *Psychosocial and Organizational Hazards: Monitoring and Control. European Series in Occupational Health no. 5.* Copenhagen: World Health Organization.

Cox, T. and Griffiths, A. (1996). Assessment of psychosocial hazards at work. In M.J. Schabracq, J.A.M. Winnubst and C.L. Cooper (eds) *Handbook of Work and Health Psychology.* New York: John Wiley.

Cox, T., Griffiths, A. and Cox, S. (1993). Stress explosion. *Health and Safety at Work*, June, 16–18.

Cox, T., Griffiths, A. and Cox, S. (1995). *Work-related Stress in Nursing: Managing the Risk.* Geneva: International Labour Organisation.

Cox, T., Griffiths, A., Barlowe, C., Randall, K., Thomson, L. and Rial-Gonzalez, E. (2000). *Organisational Interventions for Work Stress: A Risk Management Approach.* Sudbury: HSE Books.

Coyle, I.R., Sleeman, S.D. and Adams, N. (1995). Safety climate. *Journal of Safety Research*, 26, 247–54.

Crouch, D.L., Webb, D.O., Peterson, L.V., Buller, P.F. and Rollins, D.E. (1989). A critical evaluation of the Utah Power and Light Company's substance abuse management program: absenteeism, accidents and costs. In S.W. Gust and J.M. Walsh (eds) *Drugs in the Workplace: Research and Evaluation Data*, Research Monograph 91. Rockville, MD: National Institute on Drug Abuse (NIDA).

Cullen, D. (1990). *The Public Enquiry into the Piper Alpha Disaster*. London: HMSO.

Cummings, T. and Cooper, C.L. (1979). A cybernetic framework for the study of occupational stress. *Human Relations*, 32, 345–419.

Daley, A.J. and Parfitt, G. (1996). Good health – is it worth it? Mood states, physical well-being, job satisfaction and absenteeism in members and non-members of British corporate health and fitness club. *Journal of Occupational and Organizational Psychology*, 69, 121–34.

Davids, A. and Mahoney, J.T. (1957) Personality dynamics and accident proneness in an industrial setting. *Journal of Applied Psychology*, 41, 303–9.

Davis, D.R. (1958). Human errors and transport accidents. *Ergonomics*, 2, 24–33.

Davis, D.R. (1966). Railway signals passed at danger: the drivers, circumstances and psychological processes. *Ergonomics*, 9, 211–22.

Davis, J.H., Schoorman, F.D., Mayer, R.C. and Tan, H.H. (2000). The trusted general manager and business unit performance: empirical evidence of a competitive advantage. *Strategic Management Journal*, 21, 563–76.

Dedobbeleer, N. and Beland, F. (1991). A safety climate measure for construction sites. *Journal of Safety Research*, 22, 97–103.

Demmer, H. (1995). *Work Site Health Promotion: How to Go about it*. European health promotion series 4. Copenhagen: WHO.

Denison, D.R. (1996). What is the difference between organisation culture and organisation climate? A native's point of view on a decade of paradigm wars. *Academy of Management Review*, 21, 619–54.

de Rijk, A.E., Le Blanc, P.M., Schaufeli, W.B. and de Jonge, J. (1998). Active coping and need for control as moderators of the job demand-control model: effects of burnout. *Journal of Occupational and Organizational Pychology*, 71, 1–18.

Diaz, R.I. and Cabrera, D.D. (1997). Safety climate and attitude as evaluation measures of organizational safety. *Accident Analysis and Prevention*, 29, 643–50.

Domenighetti, G., D'Avanzo, B. and Bisig, B. (2000). Health effects of job insecurity among employees in the Swiss general population. *International Journal of Health Services*, 30, 477–90.

Donald, I. and Canter, D. (1994). Employee attitudes and safety in the chemical industry. *Journal of Loss Prevention in the Process Industries*, 7, 203–8.

Dorn, L. and Matthews, G. (1992). Two further studies of personality correlates of driver stress. *Personality and Individual Differences*, 13, 949–51.

Duffy, C.A. and McGoldrick, A. (1990). Stress and the bus driver in the UK transport industry. *Work and Stress*, 4, 17–27.

Dugdill, L. and Springett, J. (1994). Evaluation of workplace health promotion: a review. *Health Education Journal*, 53, 337–47.

Dupre, D. (2000). Accidents at work in the EU in 1996. *Statistics in Focus: Population and Social Conditions*, 3, 1–7.

Earnshaw, J. and Cooper, C.L. (2001). *Stress and Employer Liability*. London: Institute of Personnel and Development (IPD).

Edkins, G.D. and Pollock, C.M. (1997). The influence of sustained attention on railway accidents. *Accident Analysis and Prevention*, 29, 533–9.

Edwards, J., Baglioni, A. and Cooper, C. (1990). Stress, type-A, coping and psychological and physical symptoms: a multi-sample test of alternative models. *Human Relations*, 43, 919–56.

Elkin, A.J. and Rosch, P.J. (1990). Promoting mental health at the workplace: the prevention side of stress management. *Occupational Medicine: State of the Art Review*, 5, 739–54.

Erera-Weatherley, P.L. (1996). Coping with stress: public welfare supervisors doing their best. *Human Relations*, 49, 157–70.

European Commission (1996). *Guidance on Risk Assessment at Work*. Luxembourg: European Commission Directorate General V.

European Commission Working Time Directive (1990). Council Directive concerning certain aspects of the organization of working time. *Official Journal of the European Communities*, no. C254/4.

Evans, G.W., Palsane, M.N. and Carrere, S. (1987). Type A behavior and occupational stress: a cross-cultural study of blue-collar workers. *Journal of Personality and Social Psychology*, 52, 1002–7.

Evans, L. (1991). *Traffic Safety and the Driver*. New York: Van Nostrand Reinhold.

Eysenck, H.J. (1962). *The Structure of Human Personality*. London: Methuen.

Eysenck, H.J. (1970). The personality of drivers and pedestrians. *Medicine, Science and the Law*, 3, 416–23.

Farmer, E. (1984). Personality factors in aviation. *International Journal of Aviation Safety*, 2, 175–9.

Farmer, E. and Chambers, E.G. (1926). *A Psychological Study of Individual Differences in Accident Liability*, Industrial Fatigue Research Board Report no. 38. London: HMSO.

Fennell, D. (1988). *Investigation into the King's Cross Underground Fire*. London: HMSO.

Fergenson, P.E. (1971). The relationship between information processing and driving accident and violation record. *Human Factors*, 13, 173–6.

Ferguson, E. and Cox, T. (1997). The functional dimensions of coping scale: theory reliability and validity. *British Journal of Health Psychology*, 2, 109–29.

Fine, B.J. (1963). Introversion–extraversion and motor vehicle driver behavior. *Perceptual and Motor Skills*, 16, 95–100.

Fleming, M., Flin, R., Mearns, K. and Gordon, R. (1998). Risk perceptions of offshore workers on UK oil and gas platforms. *Risk Analysis*, 18, 103–10.

Fletcher, B.C. and Jones, F. (1993). A refutation of Karasek's demand-discretion model of occupational stress with a range of dependent measures. *Journal of Organizational Behavior*, 14, 319–30.

Flin, R. (1998). Safety culture: identifying and measuring the common features. Paper presented at the International Association of Applied Psychology (IAAP) conference, San Francisco, CA, August.

Flin, R., Mearns, K., Fleming, M. and Gordon, R. (1996). *Risk Perception and Safety in the Offshore Oil and Gas Industry (OTH 94454)*. London: HSE.

Flin, R., Mearns, K., O'Connor, R. and Bryden, R. (2000). Measuring safety climate: identifying the common features. *Safety Science*, 34, 177–92.

Fried, Y., Rowland, K.M. and Ferris, G.R. (1984). The physiological measurement of work stress: a critique. *Personnel Psychology*, 37, 583–615.

Ganster, D. and Schaubroeck, J. (1995). The moderating effects of self-esteem on the work stress-employee health relationship. In R. Crandall and P. Perrewe (eds) *Occupational Stress: A Handbook*. Washington, DC: Taylor & Francis.

Ganster, D., Schaubroeck, J., Sime, W. and Mayes, B. (1991). The nomological validity of the type A personality among adults. *Journal of Applied Psychology*, 76, 143–68.

Geller, E.S., Roberts, D.S. and Gilmore, M.R. (1996). Predicting propensity to actively care for occupational safety. *Journal of Safety Research*, 27, 1–8.

George, J. (1992). The role of personality in organisational life: issues and evidence. *Journal of Management*, 18, 185–213.

George, J.M. and Brief, A.P. (1992). Feeling good-doing good: a conceptual analysis of the mood at work–organizational spontaneity relationship. *Psychological Bulletin*, 112, 310–29.

Geurts, S. and Grundemann, R. (1999). Workplace stress and stress prevention in Europe. In M. Kompier and C. Cooper (eds) *Preventing Stress, Improving Productivity: European Case Studies in the Work-place*. London: Routledge.

Gilchrist, A.O., Bowen, K.C., Moynihan, P., Hutchings, B.W., Taylor, R.K. and Asburner, E. (1989). *An Investigation into the Causation of Signals Passed at Danger*. British Rail Internal Report. Cited in S.G. Clarke (1993) The effects of organisational communication on the safety attitudes of train drivers. Unpublished PhD thesis, University of Manchester.

Gillen, M., Baltz, D., Gassel, M., Kirsch, L. and Vaccaro, D. (2002). Perceived safety climate, job demands, and coworker support among union and non-union injured construction workers. *Journal of Safety Research*, 33, 33–51.

Glendon, A.I. (1991). Accident data analysis. *Journal of Health and Safety*, 7, 5–24.

Glendon, A.I. and Litherland, D.K. (2001). Safety climate factors, group differences and safety behaviour in road construction. *Safety Science*, 39, 157–88.

Glendon, A.I. and McKenna, E.F. (1995). *Human Safety and Risk Management*. London: Chapman and Hall.

Glendon, A.I. and Stanton, N. (1998). Safety culture: top down and bottom up approaches. Paper presented at the International Association of Applied Psychology (IAAP) conference, San Francisco, CA, August.

Goldberg, D. (1978). *Manual of the General Health Questionnaire*. London: Oxford University Press.

Goldberg, L.R. (1990). An alternative 'description of personality': the Big-Five factor structure. *Journal of Personality and Social Psychology*, 59, 1216–29.

Goodman, P.S., Devada, R. and Hughson, T.G. (1988). Groups and productivity: analyzing the effectiveness of self-managing teams. In J.P. Campbell, R.J. Campbell and Associates (eds) *Productivity in Organizations*. San Francisco, CA: Jossey-Bass.

Greenberger, D.B., Strasser, S., Cummings, L.L. and Dunham, R.B. (1989). The impact of personal control on performance and satisfaction. *Organizational Behavior and Human Decision Processes*, 43, 29–51.

Greenwood, M. and Woods, H.M. (1919). A report on the incidence of industrial accidents upon individuals with special reference to multiple accidents. In W. Haddon, E.A. Suchman and D. Klein (eds) (1964) *Accident Proneness*. New York: Harper and Row.

Greiner, B.A., Krause, N., Ragland, D.R. and Fisher, J.M. (1998). Objective stress factors, accidents, and absenteeism in transit operators: a theoretical framework and empirical evidence. *Journal of Occupational Health Psychology*, 3, 130–46.

Griffin, M.A. and Neal, A. (2000). Perceptions of safety at work: a framework for linking safety climate to safety performance, knowledge, and motivation. *Journal of Occupational Health Psychology*, 5, 347–58.

Griffin, M., Neal, A. and Rafferty, A. (2002). The influence of leadership and safety climate on safety behaviour. Paper presented at the Conference of the 25th International Congress of Applied Psychology, Singapore, July.

Griffiths, D.K. (1985). Safety attitudes of management. *Ergonomics*, 28, 61–7.

Groeneweg, J. (1992). *Controlling the Controllable: The Management of Safety*. Leiden, Netherlands: DSWO Press.

Guastello, S.J. and Guastello, J.D. (1986). The relation between the locus of control construct and involvement in traffic accidents. *Journal of Psychology*, 120, 293–7.

Guest, D.E., Peccei, R. and Thomas, A. (1994). Safety culture and safety performance: British Rail in the aftermath of the Clapham Junction disaster. Paper presented at the Bolton Business School Conference on Changing Perceptions of Risk, Bolton, UK, February.

Guilford, J.S. (1973). Prediction of accidents in a standardized home environment. *Journal of Applied Psychology*, 57, 306–13.

Guldenmund, F.W. (2000). The nature of safety culture: a review of theory and research. *Safety Science*, 34, 215–57.

Gulian, E., Matthews, G., Glendon, A.I., Davies, D.R. and Debney, L.M. (1989). Dimensions of driver stress. *Ergonomics*, 32, 585–602.

Guppy, A. and Marsden. J. (1996). Alcohol and drug misuse and the organisation. In M.J. Schabracq, J.A.M. Winnubst and C.L. Cooper (eds) *Handbook of Work and Health Psychology*. New York: John Wiley.

Haga, S. (1984) An experimental study of signal vigilance errors in train driving. *Ergonomics*, 27, 755–65.

Hale, A.R. and Hale, M. (1972). *A Review of the Industrial Accident Literature*. London: HMSO.

Hansen, C.P. (1988). Personality characteristics of the accident involved employee. *Journal of Business and Psychology*, 2, 346–65.

Hansen, C.P. (1989). A causal model of the relationship among accidents, biodata, personality and cognitive factors. *Journal of Applied Psychology*, 74, 81–90.

Hardy, G.E., Shapiro, D.A. and Borrill, C.S. (1997). Fatigue in the workforce of national health service trusts: levels of symptomatology and links with minor psychiatric disorder, demographic, occupational and work role factors. *Journal of Psychosomatic Research*, 43, 83–92.

Harrell, W.A. (1990). Perceived risk of occupational injury: control over pace of work and blue-collar versus white-collar work. *Perceptual and Motor Skills*, 70, 1351–9.

Harris, J.R. (1991). The utility of the transactional approach for occupational stress research. *Journal of Social Behaviour and Personality*, 6, 21–9.

Hart, P.M. (1994). Teacher quality of work life: integrating work experiences, psychological distress and morale. *Journal of Occupational and Organizational Psychology*, 67, 109–32.

Hart, P., Wearing, A. and Headey, B. (1995). Police stress and well-being: integrating personality, coping and daily work experiences. *Journal of Occupational and Organizational Psychology*, 68, 133–56.

Health and Safety Commission (1993). *Third Report: Organising for Safety*. ACSNI Study Group on Human Factors. London: HMSO.

Health and Safety Executive (1991). *Successful Health and Safety Management*. London: HMSO.

Health and Safety Executive (1997). *The Health and Safety Climate Survey Tool*. Sudbury: HSE Books.

Health and Safety Executive (1999). *The Costs to Britain of Workplace Accidents and Work Related Ill Health in 1995/96*. Sudbury: HSE Books.

Hemenway, D. and Solnick, S.J. (1993). Fuzzy dice, dream cars, and indecent gestures: correlates of driver behaviour. *Accident Analysis and Prevention*, 25, 161–70.

Hemingway, M. and Smith, C.S. (1999). Organisational climate and occupational stressors as predictors of withdrawal behaviours and injuries in nurses. *Journal of Occupational and Organizational Psychology*, 72, 285–99.

Herbert, R. and Landrigan, P.J. (2000). Work-related death: a continuing epidemic. *American Journal of Public Health*, 90, 541–5.

Hidden, A. (1989). *Investigation into the Clapham Junction Railway Accident*. Department of Transport, Cm 820. London: HMSO.

Highley-Marchington, C. and Cooper, C.L. (1998). *An Assessment of EAPs and Workplace Counselling in British Organizations*. Norwich: HSMO.

Hobbs, A. and Williamson, A. (2002). Skills, rules and knowledge in aircraft maintenance errors in context. *Ergonomics*, 45, 290–308.

Hockey, G.R.J., Clough, P.J. and Maule, A.I. (1996). Effects of emotional state on decision making and risk behaviour. Presented at the Risk and Human Behaviour (Economic and Social Research Council) Conference, York, UK, September.

Hofmann, D.A. and Morgeson, F.P. (1999). Safety-related behavior as a social exchange: the role of perceived organizational support and leader-member exchange. *Journal of Applied Psychology*, 84, 286–96.

Hofmann, D.A. and Stetzer, A. (1996). A cross-level investigation of factors influencing unsafe behaviours and accidents. *Personnel Psychology*, 49, 307–39.

Hofmann, D.A., Morgeson, F.P. and Gerras, S.J. (2001). When is safety my job? The moderating effect of LMX and leader safety commitment on subordinate role definition and behavior. Paper presented at the Society for Industrial and Organizational Psychology Conference, San Diego, CA.

Holcum, M.L., Lehman, W.E.K. and Simpson, D.D. (1993). Employee accidents: influences of personal characteristics, job characteristics, and substance use in jobs differing in accident potential. *Journal of Safety Research*, 24, 205–11.

Hopfl, H. (1994). Safety culture, corporate culture: organizational transformation and the commitment to safety. *Disaster Prevention and Management*, 3, 49–58.

Hough, L.M. (1992). The 'Big Five' personality variables – construct confusion: description versus prediction. *Human Performance*, 5, 139–55.

House, J.S. (1981). *Work Stress and Social Support*. Reading, MA: Addison-Wesley.

Houston, D. and Allt, S.K. (1997). Psychological distress and error making among junior house officers. *British Journal of Health Psychology*, 2, 141–51.

Hurrell, J.J. and Murphy, L. (1991). Locus of control, job demands and health. In C.L. Cooper and R. Payne (eds) *Personality and Stress: Individual Differences in the Stress Process*. Chichester: John Wiley.

INSAG (International Nuclear Safety Advisory Group) (1991). *Safety Culture*. Safety Series 75-INSAG-4. Vienna: IAEA.

International Atomic Energy Agency (IAEA) (1986). *Summary Report on the Post-Accident Review Meeting on the Chernobyl Accident*. Safety Series 75-INSAG-1. Vienna: IAEA.

International Atomic Energy Agency (IAEA) (1988). *Basic Safety Principles for Nuclear Power Plants*. Safety Series 75-INSAG-3. Vienna: IAEA.

International Labour Organisation (ILO) (1992). *Conditions of Work Digest: Preventing Stress at Work* (V. Di Martino, ed.). Geneva: ILO.

International Survey Research (ISR) (1995). *Tracking Trends: Employee Satisfaction in Europe*. London: ISR.

Israel, B.A., Baker, E.A., Goldenhar, L.M., Heaney, C.A. and Schurman, S.J. (1996). Occupational stress, safety and health: conceptual framework and principles for effective prevention interventions. *Journal of Occupational Health Psychology*, 1, 261–86.

Iversen, H. and Rundmo, T. (2002). Personality, risky driving and accident involvement. *Personality and Individual Differences*, 33, 1251–63.

Iverson, R.D. and Erwin, P.J. (1997). Predicting occupational injury: the role of affectivity. *Journal of Occupational and Organizational Psychology*, 70, 113–28.

Jackofsky, E.F. and Slocum, J.W. Jr (1988). A longitudinal study of climates. *Journal of Organizational Behaviour*, 9, 319–34.

Jackson, S.E. and Schuler, R.S (1985). A meta-analysis and conceptual critique of research on role ambiguity and role conflict in work settings. *Organisational Behaviour and Human Decision Processes*, 36, 16–78.

Jamal, M. (1999). Job stress, Type-A behaviour and well-being: a cross-cultural examination. *International Journal of Stress Management*, 6, 57–67.

Janis, I.L. (1972). *Victims of Groupthink: A Psychological Study of Foreign Policy Decisions and Fiascos*. Boston, MA: Houghton and Mifflin.

Janis, I.L. and Mann, L. (1977). *Decision-making: A Psychological Analysis of Conflict, Choice and Commitment*. New York: Free Press.

Janssens, M., Brett, J.M. and Smith, F.J. (1995). Confirmatory cross-cultural research: testing the viability of a corporation-wide safety policy. *Academy of Management Journal*, 38, 364–82.

Janzen, J.M. (1983). A study of the relationship of locus of control, age and work experience used to discriminate individuals in the saw mill industry. *Dissertation Abstracts International*, 44, 438A.

Jenkins, C., Zyzanski, S. and Rosenman, R. (1971). Progress toward validation of a computer-scored test for the Type A behaviour pattern. *Psychosomatic Medicine*, 33, 193–202.

Jenkins, R. (1991). Demographic aspects of stress. In C.L. Cooper and R. Payne (eds) *Personality and Stress: Individual Differences in the Stress Process*. Chichester: John Wiley.

Jex, S.M. (1998). *Stress and Job Performance: Theory, Research, and Implications for Managerial Practice*. Thousand Oaks, CA: Sage.

Jex, S.M. and Beehr, T.A. (1991). Emerging theoretical and method-ological issues in the study of work-related stress. *Research in Personnel and Human Resources Management*, 9, 311–65.

Jonah, B.A. (1986). Accident risk and risk-taking behaviour among young drivers. *Accident Analysis and Prevention*, 18, 255–71.

Jonah, B.A. (1997). Sensation seeking and risky driving: a review and synthesis of the literature. *Accident Analysis and Prevention*, 29, 651–65.

Jones, J.R., Hodgson, J.T. and Osman, J. (1997). *Self-reported Working Conditions in 1995: Results from a Household Survey*. Sudbury: HSE Books.

Jones, J.W. and Wuebker, L.J. (1985). Development and validation of the Safety Locus of Control Scale. *Perceptual and Motor Skills*, 61, 151–61.

Jones, J.W. and Wuebker, L.J. (1993). Safety locus of control and employees' accidents. *Journal of Business and Psychology*, 7, 449–57.

Joyce, W. and Slocum, J. (1984). Collective climate: agreement as a basis for defining aggregate climates in organisations. *Academy of Management Journal*, 27, 721–42.

Judge, T.A. (1993). Does affective disposition moderate the relationship between job satisfaction and voluntary turnover? *Journal of Applied Psychology*, 78, 395–401.

Kahn, R.L. and Byosiere, P. (1992). Stress in organisations. In M.D. Dunnette and L.M. Hough (eds) *Handbook of Industrial and Organisational Psychology*, 2nd edition, Vol. 3. Palo Alto, CA: Consulting Psychologists Press.

Karasek, R.A. (1979). Job demands, job decision latitude and mental strain: implications for job redesign. *Administrative Science Quarterly*, 24, 285–308.

Karasek, R.A. (1992). Stress prevention through work reorganisation: a summary of 19 international case studies. In International Labour Organisation, *Conditions of Work Digest: Preventing Stress at Work* (V. Di Martino, ed.). Geneva: ILO.

Karasek, R.A. and Theorell, T. (1990). *Healthy Work, Stress, Productivity, and the Reconstruction of Working Life.* New York: Basic Books.

Kaufmann, G. and Beehr, T. (1986). Interactions between job stressors and social support: some counterintuitive results. *Journal of Applied Psychology*, 71, 522–6.

Keehn, J.D. (1961). Accident tendency, avoidance learning and perceptual defense. *Australian Journal of Psychology*, 13, 157–69.

Keenan, V., Kerr, C. and Sherman, W. (1951). Psychological climate and accidents in an automobile plant. *Journal of Applied Psychology*, 35, 108–11.

Kennedy, R. and Kirwan, B. (1995). The failure mechanisms of safety culture. In A. Carnino and G. Weimann (eds) *Proceedings of the International Topical Meeting on Safety Culture in Nuclear Installations.* Vienna: American Nuclear Society of Austria.

King, J. E. (2000). White-collar reactions to job insecurity and the role of the psychological contract: implications for human resource management. *Human Resource Management*, 39, 79–91.

Kinicki, A.J., McKee, F.M. and Wade, K.J. (1996). Annual review 1991–1995: occupational health. *Journal of Vocational Behaviour*, 49, 190–220.

Kirkcaldy, B.D., Trimpop, R. and Cooper, C.L. (1997). Working hours, job stress, work satisfaction and accident rates among medical practitioners, consultants and allied personnel. *International Journal of Stress Management*, 4, 79–98.

Kirmeyer, S.L. and Dougherty, T.W. (1988). Work load, tension and coping: moderating effects of supervisor support. *Personnel Psychology*, 41, 125–39.

Kirwan, B. (1998). Safety management assessment and task analysis – a missing link? In A. Hale and M. Baram (eds) *Safety Management: The Challenge of Change.* Oxford: Elsevier.

Kivimaeki, M., Elovainio, M., Vahtera, J. and Cooper, C.L. (2001). Contingent employment, health and sickness absence. *Scandinavian Journal of Work, Environment and Health*, 27, 365–72.

Koeske, G.F., Kirk, S.A. and Koeske, R.D. (1993). Coping with job stress: which strategies work best? *Journal of Occupational and Organizational Psychology*, 66, 319–35.

Kogi, K. (1972). Repeated short indifference periods in industrial vigilance. *Journal of Human Ergology*, 1, 111–21.

Kompier, M.A.J. (1996). Job design and well-being. In M.J. Schabracq, J.A.M. Winnubst and C.L. Cooper (eds) *Handbook of Work and Health Psychology*. New York: John Wiley.

Kompier, M.A.J and Levi, L. (1993). *Stress at Work: Causes, Effects and Prevention*. Dublin: European Foundation for the Improvement of Living and Working Conditions.

Kompier, M.A.J., Geurts, S.A.E., Grundeman, R.W.M., Vink, P. and Smulders, P.G.W. (1998). Cases in stress prevention: the success of a participative and stepwise approach. *Stress Medicine*, 14, 155–68.

Kozlowski, S.W.J. and Doherty, M.L. (1989). Integration of climate and leadership: examination of a neglected issue. *Journal of Applied Psychology*, 74, 546–33.

Kunce, J.T. (1967). Vocational interests and accident proneness. *Journal of Applied Psychology*, 51, 223–5.

Lajunen, T. (2001). Personality and accident liability: are extraversion, neuroticism and psychoticism related to traffic and occupational fatalities? *Personality and Individual Differences*, 31, 1365–73.

Lajunen, T. and Parker, D. (2001). Are aggressive people aggressive drivers? A study of the relationship between self-reported general aggressiveness, driver anger and aggressive driving. *Accident Analysis and Prevention*, 33, 243–55.

Langham, M., Hole, G., Edwards, J. and O'Neil, C. (2002). An analysis of 'looked but failed to see' accidents involving parked police cars. *Ergonomics*, 45, 167–85.

Lardent, C. L. (1991). Pilots who crash: personality constructs underlying accident prone behavior of fighter pilots. *Multivariate Experimental Clinical Research*, 10, 1–25.

Lawton, R. and Parker, D. (1998). Individual differences in accident liability: a review and integrative approach. *Human Factors*, 40, 655–71.

Lazarus, R.S. (1991). Psychological stress in the workplace. *Journal of Social Behaviour and Personality*, 6, 1–13.

Leather, P.J. (1987). Safety and accidents in the construction industry: a work design perspective. *Work and Stress*, 1, 167–74.

Lee, C., Ashford, S. and Jamieson, L (1993). The effects of Type A behaviour dimensions and optimism on coping strategy, health and performance. *Journal of Organizational Behaviour*, 14, 143–57.

Lee, T. (1998). Assessment of safety culture at a nuclear reprocessing plant. *Work and Stress*, 12, 217–37.

Lee, T.W. and Johnson, D.R. (1991). The effects of work schedule and employment status on the organisational commitment and job satisfaction of full versus part time employees. *Journal of Vocational Behaviour*, 38, 204–24.

Leonard, C., Fanning, N., Attwood, J. and Buckley, M. (1998). The effect of fatigue, sleep deprivation and onerous working hours on the physical and mental well-being of pre-registration house officers. *Irish Journal of Medical Science*, 167, 22–5.

Lepore, S., Evans, G. and Schneider, M. (1991). Dynamic role of social support in the link between chronic stress and psychological distress. *Journal of Personality and Social Psychology*, 61, 899–909.

LeShan, L.L. (1952). Dynamics of accident-prone behaviour. *Psychiatry*, 15, 73–80.

Loo, R. (1979). Role of primary personality factors in the perception of traffic signs and driver violations and accidents. *Accident Analysis and Prevention*, 11, 125–7.

Lowrance, W.W. (1976). *Of Acceptable Risk*. Los Altos, CA: William Kaufmann.

Lubner, M.E. (1992). Aviation accidents, incidents, and violations: psychological predictors among United States pilots. *Dissertation Abstracts International*, 53(6–B), 3003–4.

McClain, D.L. (1995). Responses to health and safety risk in the work environment. *Academy of Management Journal*, 38, 1,726–43.

McDonough, P. (2000). Job insecurity and health. *International Journal of Health Services*, 30, 453–76.

McFarlane, L.J. (1997). An audit of stress, job satisfaction and general psychological health in a leading national retail organization. Unpublished MSc dissertation, School of Management, UMIST, Manchester.

McKenna, F.P. (1983). Accident proneness: a conceptual analysis. *Accident Analysis and Prevention*, 15, 65–71.

McKenna, F.P., Duncan, J. and Brown, I.D. (1986). Cognitive abilities and safety on the road: a re-examination of individual differences in dichotic listening and search for embedded figures. *Ergonomics*, 29, 649–63.

Magnavita, N., Narda, R., Sani, L., Carbone, A., De Lorenzo, G. and Sacco, A. (1997). Type A behaviour pattern and traffic accidents. *British Journal of Medical Psychology*, 70, 103–7.

Manning, M.R. and Osland, J.S. (1989). The relationship between absenteeism and stress. *Work and Stress*, 3, 223–35.

Marmot, M.G., Feeney, A., Shipley, M., North, F. and Syme, S.L. (1995). Sickness absence as a measure of health status and functioning: from the UK Whitehall II study. *Journal of Epidemiology and Community Health*, 49, 124–30.

Maruyama, S., Kohno, K. and Morimoto, K. (1995). A study of preventive medicine in relation to mental health among middle-management employees (Part 2) – effects of long working hours on lifestyles, perceived stress and working-life satisfaction among white-collar middle-management employees. *Japanese Journal of Hygiene*, 50, 849–60.

Matthews, G. (1993). Cognitive processes in driver stress. In *Proceedings of the 1993 International Congress of Health Psychology*. Tokyo: International Congress of Health Psychology.

Matthews, G., Dorn, L. and Glendon, A.I. (1991). Personality correlates of driver stress. *Personality and Individual Differences*, 12, 535–49.

Matthews, G., Sparkes, T.J. and Bygrave, H.M. (1996). Attentional overload, stress, and simulated driving performance. *Human Performance*, 9, 77–101.

Matthews, G., Dorn, L., Hoyes, T.W., Davies, D.R., Glendon, A.I. and Taylor, R.G. (1998). Driver stress and performance on a driving simulator. *Human Factors*, 40, 136–49.

Matthews, G., Tsuda, A., Xin, G. and Ozeki, Y. (1999). Individual differences in driver stress vulnerability in a Japanese sample. *Ergonomics*, 42, 401–15.

Mayer, R.C., Davis, J.H. and Schoorman, F.D. (1995). An integrative model of organisational trust. *Academy of Management Review*, 20, 709–34.

Mayer, R.E. and Treat, J.R. (1977). Psychological, social and cognitive characteristics of high risk drivers: a pilot study. *Accident Analysis and Prevention*, 9, 1–8.

Meadows, M.L., Stradling, S.G. and Lawson, S. (1998). The role of social deviance and violations in predicting road traffic accidents in a sample of young offenders. *British Journal of Psychology*, 89, 417–31.

Mearns, K., Flin, R., Fleming, M. and Gordon, R. (1998). Measuring safety climate on offshore installations. *Work and Stress*, 12, 238–54.

Mearns, K., Whitaker, S.M. and Flin, R. (2003). Safety climate, safety management practice and safety performance in offshore environments. *Safety Science*, 41, 641–80.

Melamed, S., Luz, J., Najenson, T., Jucha, E. and Green, M. (1989). Ergonomic stress levels, personal characteristics, accident occurrence and sickness absence among factory workers. *Ergonomics*, 32, 1101–10.

Melia, J.L., Tomas, J.M., Oliver, A. and Islas, M.E. (1992). Organizational and psychological variables as antecedents of work safety: a causal model. Paper presented at the Safety and Well-Being at Work conference, Loughborough, UK, November.

Merritt, A.C. and Helmreich, R.L. (1996). Creating and sustaining a safety culture. *CRM Advocate*, 1, 8–12.

Michaels, C.E. and Spector, P.E. (1982). Causes of employee turnover: a test of the Mobley, Griffeth, Hand and Meglino model. *Journal of Applied Psychology*, 67, 53–9.

Miner, J.B. and Brewer, J.F. (1983). The management of ineffective performance. In M.D. Dunnette (ed.) *Handbook of Industrial and Organisational Psychology*. New York: John Wiley.

Monk, T.H., Folkard, S. and Wedderburn, A.I. (1996). Maintaining safety and high performance on shiftwork. *Applied Ergonomics*, 27, 17–23.

Moorhead, G., Ference, R. and Neck, C. P. (1991). Group think fiascoes continue: space shuttle Challenger and a revised groupthink framework. *Human Relations*, 44, 539.

Moos, R.H. and Insel, P.M. (1974). *Manual for the Work Environment Scale*. Palo Alto, CA: Consulting Psychologists Press.

Morrow, P.C. and Crum, M.R. (1998). The effects of perceived and objective safety risk on employee outcomes. *Journal of Vocational Behaviour*, 53, 300–13.

Mossink, J. and Licher, F. (1998) *Costs and Benefits of Occupational Safety and Health 1997*. Amsterdam: NIA–TNO.

Moyle, P. (1995). The role of negative affectivity in the stress process: tests of alternative models. *Journal of Organizational Behaviour*, 16, 647–68.

Moyle, P. and Parkes, K. (1999). The effects of transition stress: a relocation study. *Journal of Organizational Behavior*, 20, 625–46.

Mullarkey, S., Jackson, P.R., Wall, T.D., Wilson, J.R. and Grey-Taylor, S.M. (1997). The impact of technology characteristics and job control on worker mental health. *Journal of Organizational Behavior*, 18, 471–89.

Murphy, L.R. (1988). Workplace interventions for stress reduction and prevention. In C.L. Cooper and R. Payne (eds) *Causes, Coping and Consequences of Stress at Work*. New York: John Wiley.

Murphy, L.R., DuBois, D. and Hurrell, J.J. (1986). Accident reduction through stress management. *Journal of Business and Psychology*, 1, 5–18.

National Institute of Occupational Safety and Health (NIOSH) (1986). *Proposed National Strategies for the Prevention of Leading Work-related Disease and Injuries*. Cincinnati, OH: NIOSH.

National Institute of Occupational Safety and Health (NIOSH) (1996). *National Occupational Research Agenda (NORA)*. Available at: http://www.cdc.gov/niosh/nora.html

National Occupational Health and Safety Commission (2000). *Compendium of Workers' Compensation Statistics, Australia, 1998–1999*. Canberra: Commonwealth of Australia.

National Safety Council (2001). *Report on Injuries in America 2001*. Available at: http://www.nsc.org/library/rept2000.htm

Neal, A., Griffin, M.A. and Hart, P.M. (2000). The impact of organisational climate on safety climate and individual behaviour. *Safety Science*, 34, 99–110.

Neck, C.P. and Cooper, K.H. (2000). The fit executive: exercise and diet guidelines for enhancing performance. *Academy of Management Executive*, 14, 72–83.

Newbold, E.M. (1926). *A Contribution to the Study of the Human Factor in the Causation of Accidents*, Industrial Fatigue Research Board Report no. 34. London: HMSO.

Newbold, E.M. (1927). Practical applications of the statistics of repeated events. *Journal of the Royal Statistical Society*, 92, 487–535.

Newton, T.J. and Keenan, A. (1990). The moderating effects of the Type A behaviour pattern and locus of control upon the relationship between change in job demands and change in psychological strain. *Human Relations*, 43, 1229–55.

Niskanen, T. (1994). Safety climate in the road administration. *Safety Science*, 17, 237–55.

Norman, D.A. (1981). Categorisation of action slips. *Psychological Review*, 88, 1–15.

Norris, F.H., Matthews, B.A. and Riad, J.K. (2000). Characterological, situational, and behavioral risk factors for motor vehicle accidents: a prospective examination. *Accident Analysis and Prevention*, 32, 505–15.

O'Dea, A. and Flin, R. (2000). Site managers and safety leadership in the offshore oil and gas industry. *Safety Science*, 37, 39–57.

OECD (1999). *Implementing the OECD Job Strategy: Assessing Performance and Policy*. Paris: OECD.

Oliver, A., Tomas, J.M. and Melia, J.L. (1993). A psychometric study of a new measure of safety climate. Paper presented at the Safety and Well-Being at Work conference, Loughborough, UK, November.

Oliver, A., Cheyne, A., Tomas, J.M. and Cox, S. (2002). The effects of organizational and individual factors on occupational accidents. *Journal of Occupational and Organizational Psychology*, 75, 473–88.

Pablo, A.L. (1997). Reconciling predictions of decision making under risk. *Journal of Managerial Psychology*, 12, 4–20.

Paoli, P. (1997). *Second European Survey for the European Foundation for the Improvement of Living and Working Conditions*. Luxembourg: European Foundation.

Parker, D.F. and DeCotiis, T.A. (1983). Organisational determinants of job stress. *Organisational Behaviour and Human Performance*, 32, 160–77.

Parker, D., Manstead, A.S., Stradling, S.G., Reason, J.T. and Baxter, J. (1992). Intention to commit driving violations: an application of the theory of planned behavior. *Journal of Applied Psychology*, 77, 94–101.

Parker, D., Reason, J.T., Manstead, A.S.R. and Stradling, S. (1995). Driving errors, driving violations and accident involvement. *Ergonomics*, 38, 1036–48.

Parker, J.W. (1953). Psychological and personal history data related to accident records of commercial truck drivers. *Journal of Applied Psychology*, 37, 317–20.

Parker, S.K., Axtell, C.M. and Turner, N. (2001). Designing a safer workplace: importance of job autonomy, communication quality and supportive supervisors. *Journal of Occupational Health Psychology*, 6, 211–18.

Parkes, K.R. (1990). Coping, negative affectivity, and the work environment: additive and interactive predictors of mental health. *Journal of Applied Psychology*, 75, 399–409.

Parkes, K., Mendham, C. and von Rabenau, C. (1994). Social support and the demand-discretion model of job stress: tests of additive and interactive effects in two samples. *Journal of Vocational Behaviour*, 44, 91–113.

Payne, R. (1988). Individual differences in the study of occupational stress. In C. Cooper and R. Payne (eds) *Causes, Coping and Consequences of Stress at Work*. New York: John Wiley.

Pearce, J.L. (1993). Toward an organizational behaviour of contract labourers: their psychological involvement and effects on employee co-worker. *Academy of Management Journal*, 36, 1082–96.

Perry, A.R. (1986). Type A behaviour pattern and motor vehicle drivers' behaviour. *Perceptual and Motor Skills*, 63, 875–8.

Pestonjee, D.M. and Singh, U.B. (1980). Neuroticism–extroversion as correlates of accident occurrence. *Accident Analysis and Prevention*, 12, 201–4.

Pidgeon, N.F. (1991). Safety culture and risk management in organizations. *Journal of Cross-Cultural Psychology*, 22, 129–40.

Pidgeon, N.F. (1998). Safety culture: key theoretical issues. *Work and Stress*, 12, 202–16.

Porter, C.S. (1988) Accident proneness: a review of the concept. In D.J. Oborne (ed.) *International Reviews of Ergonomics: Current Trends in Human Factors Research and Practices*, vol. 2. London: Taylor and Francis.

Porter, C.S. and Corlett, E.N. (1989). Performance differences of individuals classified by questionnaire as accident prone or non-accident prone. *Ergonomics*, 32, 317–33.

Powell, P.I., Hale, M., Martin. J. and Simon, M. (1971). *2000 Accidents: A Shop Floor Study of their Causes (Report no. 21)*. London: National Institute of Industrial Psychology.

Probst, T.M. and Brubaker, T.L. (2001). The effects of job insecurity on employee safety outcomes: cross-sectional and longitudinal explorations. *Journal of Occupational Health Psychology*, 6, 139–59.

Quick, J. and Quick, J. (1984). *Organizational Stress and Preventative Management*. New York: McGraw-Hill.

Rasmussen, J. (1982). Human errors: a taxonomy for describing human malfunction in industrial installations. *Journal of Occupational Accidents*, 4, 311–35.

Reason, J. (1990). *Human Error*. Cambridge: Cambridge University Press.

Reason, J. (1993). Managing the management risk: new approaches to organizational safety. In B. Wilpert and T. Qvale (eds) *Reliability and Safety in Hazardous Work Systems*. Hove: Lawrence Erlbaum.

Reason, J. (1995). A systems approach to organizational error. *Ergonomics*, 38, 1708–21.

Reason, J. (1997). *Managing the Risks of Organizational Accidents*. Aldershot: Ashgate.

Reason, J. (1998). Achieving a safety culture: theory and practice. *Work and Stress*, 12, 293–306.

Reason, J.T., Manstead, A.S.R., Stradling, S.G., Baxter, J.S. and Campbell, K. (1990). Errors and violations on the road: a real distinction? *Ergonomics*, 33, 1315–32.

Reason, J.T., Parker, D. and Free, R. (1994). *Bending the Rules: The Varieties, Origins and Management of Safety Violations*. Leiden, Netherlands: Rijks Universiteit Leiden.

Reason, J., Parker, D. and Lawton, R. (1998). Organizational controls and safety: the varieties of rule-related behaviour. *Journal of Occupational and Organizational Psychology*, 71, 289–304.

Rees, D. and Cooper, C.L. (1992). Occupational stress in Health Service workers in the UK. *Stress Medicine*, 8, 79–90.

Reynard, W.D., Billings, C.E., Cheaney, E.S. and Hardy, R. (1986). *The Development of the NASA Aviation Safety Reporting System*. Reference Publication 1114. Moffett Field, CA: National Aeronautics and Space Administration.

Robertson, I. and Clarke, S. (1999). Personality and accident involvement: implications for personnel selection. Paper presented at the SIOP International Conference, Atlanta, GA, April.

Robertson, I. and Clarke, S. (2002). Personality and accidents in high-risk occupations: a meta-analysis. Paper presented at the Conference of the 25th International Congress of Applied Psychology, Singapore, July.

Robertson, I.T., Baron, H., Gibbons, P., MacIver, R. and Nyfield, G. (2000). Conscientiousness and managerial performance. *Journal of Occupational and Organisational Psychology*, 73, 171–80.

Rosa, R.R. (1995). Extended work shifts and excessive fatigue. *Journal of Sleep Research*, 4, 51–6.

Rosa, R.R., Colligan, M.J. and Lewis, P. (1989). Extended work days: effects of 8 hour and 12 hour rotating schedules on performance, subjective, alertness, sleep patterns and psychosocial variables. *Work and Stress*, 3, 21–32.

Roy, G.S. and Choudhary, R.K. (1985). Driver control as a factor in road safety. *Asian Journal of Psychology and Education*, 16, 33–7.

Royal Society (1983). *Risk Assessment: A Study Group Report*. London: Royal Society.

Rundmo, T. (1995). Perceived risk, safety status, and job stress among injured and noninjured employees on offshore petroleum installations. *Journal of Safety Research*, 26, 87–97.

Sah, A.P. (1989). Personality characteristics of accident free and accident involved Indian railway drivers. *Journal of Personality and Clinical Studies*, 5, 203–6.

Salgado, J.F. (1997). The five factor model of personality and job performance in the European Community. *Journal of Applied Psychology*, 82, 30–43.

Schabracq, M., Winnubst, J. and Cooper, C. (1996). *Handbook of Work and Health Psychology*. New York: John Wiley.

Schaubroeck, J. and Fink, L. (1998). Facilitating and inhibiting effects of job control and social support on stress outcomes and role behaviour: a contingency model. *Journal of Organizational Behavior*, 19, 167–95.

Schein, E.H. (1985). *Organizational Culture and Leadership*. San Francisco, CA: Jossey-Bass.

Schein, E.H. (1992). *Organizational Culture and Leadership*, 2nd edn. San Francisco, CA: Jossey-Bass.

Schneider, B. (1975). Organizational climates: an essay. *Personnel Psychology*, 28, 447–79.

Schneider, B. and Rentsch, J. (1988). Managing climates and cultures: a futures perspective. In J. Hage (ed.) *Futures of Organizations: Innovating to Adapt Strategy and Human Resources to Rapid Technological Change*. Lexington, MA: Lexington Books.

Schriesheim, C.A., Castro, S.L. and Cogliser, C.C. (1999). Leader–member exchange (LMX) research: a comprehensive review of theory, measurement, and data-analytic practices. *Leadership Quarterly*, 10, 63–114.

Selzer, M.L., Rogers, J.E. and Kern, S. (1968). Fatal accidents: the role of psychopathology, social stress and acute disturbance. *American Journal of Psychiatry*, 124, 1028–36.

Semmer, N. (1996). Individual differences, work stress and health. In M. Schabracq, J. Winnubst and C. Cooper (eds) *Handbook of Work and Health Psychology*. New York: John Wiley.

Senge, P.M. (1990). *The Fifth Discipline: The Art and Practice of the Learning Organisation*. London: Century Business.

Senneck, C.R. (1975). Over three day absences and safety. *Applied Ergonomics*, 6, 147–53.

Shamir, B. (1995). Social distance and charisma: theoretical notes and an exploratory study. *Leadership Quarterly*, 6, 19–47.

Shannon, H.S., Mayr, J. and Haines, T. (1997). Overview of the relationship between organizational and workplace factors and injury rates. *Safety Science*, 26, 201–17.

Shaw, L. (1965). The practical use of projective personality tests as accident predictors. *Traffic Safety Research Review*, 9, 34–72.

Shaw, L. and Sichel, H.S. (1971). *Accident Proneness*. Oxford: Pergamon.

Sheen, Mr Justice (1987). *MV Herald of Free Enterprise Report of Court No. 8074 Formal Investigation*. London: HMSO.

Sherry, P. (1991). Person–environment fit and accident prediction. *Journal of Business and Psychology*, 5, 411–16.

Sigman, A. (1992). The state of corporate health care. *Personnel Management*, February, 47–61.

Sims, M.T., Graves, R.J. and Simpson, G.C. (1984). Mineworkers' scores for the Rotter Internal–External Locus of Control Scale. *Journal of Occupational Psychology*, 57, 327–29.

Sitkin, S.B. and Weingart, L.R. (1995). Determinants of risky decision-making behaviour: a test of the mediating role of risk perceptions and propensity. *Academy of Management Journal*, 38, 1573–92.

Smeed, R.J. (1960). Proneness of drivers to road accidents. *Nature*, 186, 273–5.

Smiley, A.M. (1990). The Hinton train disaster. *Accident Analysis and Prevention*, 22, 443–55.

Smith, D.I. and Kirkham, R.W. (1981). Relationship between some personality characteristics and driving record. *British Journal of Social Psychology*, 20, 229–31.

Smith, D.L. and Heckert, T.M. (1998). Personality characteristics and traffic accidents of college students. *Journal of Safety Research*, 29, 163–9.

Smith, M.J., Cohen, H.H. and Cohen, A. (1978). Characteristics of a successful safety program. *Journal of Safety Research*, 10, 5–15.

Sokejima, S. and Kagamimori, S. (1998). Working hours as a risk factor for acute myocardial infarction in Japan: case-control study. *British Medical Journal*, 317, 775–80.

Sparks, K. and Cooper, C.L. (1999). Occupational differences in the work–strain relationship: towards the use of situation-specific models. *Journal of Occupational and Organizational Psychology*, 72, 219–29.

Sparks, K., Cooper, C., Fried, Y. and Shirom, A. (1997). The effects of hours of work on health: a meta-analytic review. *Journal of Occupational and Organizational Psychology*, 70, 391–408.

Sparks, K., Faragher, B. and Cooper, C.L. (2001). Well-being and occupational health in the 21st century workplace. *Journal of Occupational and Organizational Psychology*, 74, 489–509.

Spector, P.E. (1986). Perceived control by employees: a meta-analysis of studies concerning autonomy and participation at work. *Human Relations*, 39, 1005–16.

Spector, P.E. (2000). A control theory of the job stress process. In C.L. Cooper (ed.) *Theories of Organisational Stress*. New York: Oxford University Press.

Spector, P.E. and O'Connell, B.J. (1994). The contribution of personality traits, negative affectivity, locus of control and Type A to the subsequent reports of job stressors and job strains. *Journal of Occupational and Organizational Psychology*, 67, 1–11.

Spector, P., Zapf, D., Chen, P. and Frese, M. (2000). Why negative affectivity should not be controlled in job stress research: don't throw the baby out with the bath water. *Journal of Organizational Behavior*, 21, 79–95.

Stallones, L. and Kraus, J.F. (1993). The occurrence and epidemiologic features of alcohol-related occupational injuries. *Addiction*, 88, 945–51.

Staw, B.M. and Barsade, S.G. (1993). Affect and managerial performance: a test of the sadder-but-wiser vs. happier and smarter hypotheses. *Administrative Science Quarterly*, 38, 304–31.

Steffy, B.D., Jones, J.W., Murphy, L.R. and Kunz, L. (1986). A demonstration of the impact of stress abatement programs on reducing employees' accidents and their costs. *American Journal of Health Promotion*, 1, 25–32.

Suchman, E.A. (1970). Accidents and social deviance. *Journal of Health and Social Behaviour*, 11, 4–15.

Suhr, V.W. (1961). Personality and driving efficiency. *Perceptual and Motor Skills*, 12, 34.

Sullman, M.J.M, Meadows, M.L. and Pajo, K.B. (2002). Aberrant driving behaviours amongst New Zealand truck drivers. *Transportation Research Part F*, 3, 217–32.

Sutherland, V.J. and Cooper, C.L. (1986). *Man and Accidents Offshore*. London: Lloyds List.

Sutherland, V.J. and Cooper, C.L. (1990). *Understanding Stress*. London: Chapman and Hall.

Sutherland, V. and Cooper, C.L. (1991). *Stress and Accidents in the Offshore Oil and Gas Industry*. Houston, TX: Gulf Publishing.

Sutherland, V. and Cooper, C.L. (2003). *De-stressing Doctors: A Self-management Guide*. London: Butterworth-Heinemann.

Terra, N. (1995). The prevention of job stress by redesigning jobs and implementing self-regulating teams. In L.R. Murphy, J.J. Hurrell, S.L. Sauter and G.P. Keita (eds) *Job Stress Interventions*. Washington, DC: American Psychological Association.

Tett, R.P., Jackson, D.N. and Rothstein, M. (1991). Personality measures as predictors of job performance: a meta-analytic review. *Personnel Psychology*, 44, 703–42.

Thompson, R.C., Hilton, T.F. and Witt, L.A. (1998). Where the safety rubber meets the shop floor: a confirmatory model of management influence on workplace safety. *Journal of Safety Research*, 29, 15–24.

Toft, B. (1993). Behavioural aspects of risk management. Paper presented at the Association of Risk Managers in Industry and Commerce Annual Conference. *Conference Proceedings*. London: AIRMIC.

Toft, B. and Reynolds, S. (1994). *Learning from Disasters: A Management Approach*. Oxford: Butterworth-Heinemann.

Tomas, J.M. and Oliver, A. (1995). The perceived effect of safety climate on occupational accidents. Paper presented at the Work and Well-Being Conference, Nottingham, UK, December.

Tomas, J.M., Melia, J.L. and Oliver, A. (1999). A cross-validation of a structural equation model of accidents: organizational and psychological variables as predictors of work safety. *Work and Stress*, 13, 49–58.

Townsend, J., Phillips, J.S. and Elkins, T.J. (2000). Employee retaliation: the neglected consequence of poor leader–member exchange relations. *Journal of Occupational Health Psychology*, 5, 457–63.

Trimpop, R., Kirkcaldy, B., Athanasou, J. and Cooper, C. (2000). Individual differences in working hours, work perceptions and accident rates in veterinary surgeries. *Work and Stress*, 14, 181–8.

Trommelen, M. (1991). Causes of and backgrounds to human error in accidents at the nylon-plant. Internal report, Leiden University. Cited by J. Groeneweg (1994) *Controlling the Uncontrollable*. Leiden, Netherlands: DSWO Press.

Turner, B.A. (1978). *Man-Made Disasters*. London: Wykeham.

Turner, B.A. (1991). The development of a safety culture. *Chemistry and Industry*, April, 241–3.

Turner, B.A. (1994). Causes of disaster: sloppy management. *British Journal of Management*, 5, 215–19.

Turner, B.A., Pidgeon, N., Blockley, D. and Toft, B. (1989). Safety culture: its importance in future risk management. Position paper for the Second World Bank Workshop on Safety Control and Risk Management, Karlstad, Sweden, November.

Underwood, G., Chapman, P., Wright, S. and Crundall, D. (1999). Anger while driving. *Transportation Research Part F*, 2, 55–68.

US Bureau of the Census (2000). *Statistical Abstract of the United States: 2000*. Washington, DC: US Bureau of the Census.

Vahtera, J., Kivimaki, M. and Pentti, J. (1997). Effect of organisational downsizing on health of employees. *Lancet*, 350, 1124–8.

Van der Flier, H. and Schoonman, W. (1988). Railway signals passed at danger: situational and personal factors underlying stop signal abuse. *Applied Ergonomics*, 19, 135–41.

Van der Schaaf, T.W. (1991). A framework for designing near miss management systems. In T.W. van der Schaaf, D.A. Lucas and A.R. Hale (eds) *Near Miss Reporting as a Safety Tool*. Oxford: Butterworth-Heinemann.

Varonen, U. and Mattila, M. (2000). The safety climate and its relationship to safety practices, safety of the work environment and occupational accidents in eight wood-processing companies. *Accident Analysis and Prevention*, 32, 761–9.

Vavrik, J. (1997). Personality and risk-taking: a brief report on adolescent male drivers. *Journal of Adolescence*, 20, 461–5.

Vredenburgh, A.G. (2002). Organizational safety: which management practices are most effective in reducing employee injury rates? *Journal of Safety Research*, 33, 259–76.

Wagenaar, W. (1992). Risk-taking and accident causation. In J.F. Yates (ed.) *Risk-taking Behaviour*. Chichester: John Wiley.

Wagenaar, W. and Groeneweg, J. (1987). Accidents at sea: multiple causes and impossible consequences. *International Journal of Man-Machine Studies*, 27, 587–98.

Waring, A. (1996). *Safety Management Systems*. London: Chapman and Hall.

Waring, A.E. and Glendon, A.I. (1998). *Management, Risk and Change*. London: Chapman and Hall.

Watson, B. and Clark, L.A. (1984). Negative affectivity: the disposition to experience aversive emotional states. *Psychological Bulletin*, 96, 465–90.

Watts, W. and Cooper, C.L. (1998). *Stop the World: Finding a Way through the Pressures of Life*. Bidford-on-Avon, UK: Hodder and Stoughton.

Webb, G.R., Redman, S., Wilkinson, C. and Sanson-Fisher, R.W. (1989). Filtering effects in reporting work injuries. *Accident Analysis and Prevention*, 21, 115–23.

West, R., Elander, J. and French, D. (1993). Mild social deviance, Type-A behaviour pattern and decision making style as predictors of self-reported driving style and traffic accident risk. *British Journal of Psychology*, 84, 207–20.

Wharton, F. (1992). Risk management: basic concepts and general principles. In J. Ansell and F. Wharton (eds) *Risk: Analysis, Assessment and Management*. Chichester: John Wiley.

Williams, S. and Cooper, C.L. (1996). *Pressure Management Indicator*. Harrogate: RAD Ltd.

Williams, S. and Cooper, C.L. (1997). The Occupational Stress Indicator. In C.P. Zalaquett and R.J. Wood (eds) *Evaluating Stress: A Book of Resources*. Lanham, MD: Scarecrow Press.

Williams, S. and Narendran, S. (1999). Determinants of managerial risk: exploring personality and cultural influences. *Journal of Social Psychology*, 139, 102–25.

Williamson, A.M., Feyer, A-M., Cairns, D. and Biancotti, D. (1997). The development of a measure of safety climate: the role of safety perceptions and attitudes. *Safety Science*, 25, 15–27.

Wilpert, B. and Klumb, P. (1993). Social dynamics, organization and management: factors contributing to system safety. In B. Wilpert and T. Qvale (eds) *Reliability and Safety in Hazardous Work Systems*. Hove: Lawrence Erlbaum.

Witt, L.A., Hellman, C. and Hilton, T.F. (1994). Management influences on perceived safety. Paper presented at the annual meeting of the American Psychological Society, San Francisco, CA.

Wolfgang, A.P. (1988). Job stress in the health professions: a study of physicians, nurses and pharmacists. *Behavioural Medicine*, 14, 43–7.

Work Family Directions (1993). *Workplace Flexibility: A Strategy for Doing Business*. Boston, MA: Work Family Directions.

Worrall, L. and Cooper, C.L. (1998). *Quality of Working Life 1998 Survey of Managers' Changing Experiences*. London: Institute of Management.

Yule, S. (2002). Do transformational leaders lead safer businesses? Paper presented at the conference of the 25th International Congress of Applied Psychology, Singapore, July.

Zalaquett, C.P. and Wood, R.J. (1997). *Evaluating Stress: A Book of Resources*. Lanham, MD: Scarecrow Press.

Zohar, D. (1980). Safety climate in industrial organizations: theoretical and applied implications. *Journal of Applied Psychology*, 65, 96–102.

Zohar, D. (2000). A group-level model of safety climate: testing the effect of group climate in microaccidents in manufacturing jobs. *Journal of Applied Psychology*, 85, 587–96.

Zohar, D. (2002a). The effects of leadership dimensions, safety climate, and assigned priorities on minor injuries in work groups. *Journal of Organizational Behavior*, 23, 75–92.

Zohar, D. (2002b). Modifying supervisory practices to improve sub-unit safety: a leadership-based intervention model. *Journal of Applied Psychology*, 87, 156–63.

Zohar, D. (2003). The influence of leadership and climate in occupational health and safety. In D.A. Hofmann and L.E. Tetrick (eds) *Individual and Organizational Health*. San Francisco, CA: Jossey-Bass.

Zuckerman, M. (1979). *Sensation Seeking: Beyond the Optimal Level of Arousal*. Hillsdale, NJ: Lawrence Erlbaum.

Index